FINANCING

OPPORTUNITY

FINANCING

OPPORTUNITY

NORBERT J. MICHEL AND JENNIFER J. SCHULP

Hardcover ISBN: 978-1-964524-56-6
Paperback ISBN: 978-1-964524-52-8
eBook ISBN: 978-1-964524-53-5
Audiobook ISBN: 978-1-964524-54-2

Cover design by Spencer Fuller and Molly von Borstel, Faceout Studio.

Printed in the United States.

CATO INSTITUTE
1000 Massachusetts Ave. NW
Washington, DC 20001
www.cato.org

Contents

Contents

Chapter 1

Introduction

In the 1930s, John Maynard Keynes, one of the world's most famous economists, compared America's financial markets to a casino. Now, nearly 100 years later, financial market critics still promote that same theme. Politicians and pundits—including Tucker Carlson, Sohrab Ahmari, and Sens. Marco Rubio (R-FL), Elizabeth Warren (D-MA), and Bernie Sanders (I-VT)—regularly attack the financial industry as harmful and wasteful.

Do they have a case? Are financial markets ruinous dens of speculation that add little to the nation's economy? Popular movies like *The Wolf of Wall Street* and *The Big Short* certainly make it seem so.

But could the story have another side? It is undeniable, after all, that Americans have created unparalleled wealth and prosperity during the past 250-plus years. Could financial markets be at least partly responsible for this achievement?

From the nation's founding, financial markets grew right along with the rest of America. In the 1990s, this relationship prompted another famous economist, Merton Miller, to observe that whether financial markets contribute to economic growth is too obvious for serious discussion.

We agree that the answer is obvious, but we regularly encounter people who disagree with us—sometimes passionately—so we wrote this book. It documents the benefits of financial markets, but it also demonstrates that Americans have *always* had a love–hate relationship with financial markets.

In fact, financial markets have been blamed for society's problems for thousands of years, long before there was a United States. This phenomenon is not too surprising because human beings suffer real hardships when they lose money. Unfortunately, the hardships make for great politics, and the *benefits* of financial markets are often an afterthought.

During the past several election cycles, for instance, critics have attacked virtually every aspect of American finance—the private equity industry; the practices of repurchasing corporate shares, conducting short sales, and buying futures and options; and even the most basic trading of stocks and bonds. But those critics are doing little more than repeating the endlessly recycled critique that financial markets facilitate too much "speculation" and too little of the "real" investments that people need.

This idea is not just endlessly recycled, it is also deeply flawed. Investing in "real" assets is speculative just like investing in financial assets. Furthermore, investing in "real" assets for the sake of investing in something tangible can be *more* wasteful than investing in financial assets.

It would make no sense, for example, to invest $1 billion to boost American tractor production by 20 percent if there is no need for so many more tractors. The result would be an enormous waste of resources, idle machines, and untold amounts of goods and services that human beings would have to live without because so many resources went into building tractors instead.

On the other hand, $1 billion in stock trades could provide long-term employment opportunities and bolster production of all kinds of goods and services with as little waste as possible. Even though these stock trades do not directly invest in any "real" assets, the activity could easily be *more* productive than investing in a tractor factory. Moreover, before an observer learns the outcomes of these investment alternatives—boosting tractor production versus stock trades—there is no objective way to determine whether one is more speculative than the other, or whether one is "good" or "bad" speculation.

All investments are speculative, and even those that do not raise money for capital goods (goods used to produce things, such as machines, equipment, buildings, etc.) still indirectly contribute to capital development. Some financial activities have less influence than others on capital goods, but this fact does not justify preventing people from undertaking certain investments. Worse, setting up a legal framework so people make only "good" investments is rife with problems.

For starters, no objective way exists to decide on the right criteria for making such judgments.

One alternative, of course, is to allow people to decide on their own which investments are most valuable—that is, allow markets to decide. This allows millions of people to weigh in on the value of all kinds of investments. Allowing markets to decide does not mean everyone will always be "right," but it does mean that when most people think an investment is worthwhile, it will be easier to undertake (and less worthwhile investments will be more difficult to pursue).

Another alternative is to allow a small group of people—either members of Congress or employees of a federal agency, for example—to make these decisions for everyone else. In this scenario, government officials would decide for everyone else which investments are "too speculative," or which ones do not produce enough value. It would be their subjective views, rather than those of people who would put their own livelihoods at risk, that determine which investments people can make.

We wrote this book because we think the latter approach is the wrong one. It's harmful to economic growth and decreases prosperity but, more importantly, it's harmful to a free society. It ultimately makes everyone dependent on a small group of people who cannot possibly know the best way for everyone else to earn a living. Put differently, the more control people give up over their money, the less control they have over what kind of life they have.

As our book documents, many modern critics of finance *want* this outcome, and they justify extreme levels of government control in the name of safety and stability. History has already shown, though, that this kind of legal and regulatory framework for financial markets does not produce safety and stability. It does the opposite: it makes financial markets more fragile.

Over time, this fragility has resulted in an ever-expanding regulatory framework, one with so many rules that it's now difficult to comprehend. Regulators now dictate the details of many basic financial activities for banks and nonbanks alike. That approach has repeatedly failed to deliver stability, yet critics regularly call for more of the same.

We wrote this book because American financial markets have been constantly inching toward full-fledged government-directed financial markets, and few people realize it. Unfortunately, too many people in the financial industry are happy to deal with more regulation and government support, so this slow march away from free enterprise is partly their own fault. But despite the short-term gains that existing firms frequently get from accepting this kind of deal, most Americans suffer the long-term consequences. And the growth of the regulatory regime has continued during the past century regardless of the political party in charge of the federal government.

A far better approach is to shift away from a regulatory framework that requires federal officials to make decisions for people, and toward one that protects them from fraudulent behavior. Getting to such a world will be a Herculean task, but anyone who wants to improve financial markets must start somewhere.

So we wrote this book.

Box 1.1: The federal government dominates financial markets

Contrary to popular myth, US financial markets are far from an unfettered free-for-all. The trend in US financial markets during the past century is toward *greater* regulation.[a] Between 1999 and the 2008 financial crisis, for example, federal financial regulators issued 7,100 pages of regulations for more than 800 separate rules.[b] Federal outlays for banking and financial regulation increased from $190 million in 1960 to $1.9 billion in 2000, while federal staff rose from approximately 2,500 employees to more than 13,000.[c]

And it's not just regulation—in some areas of finance, government is an active player. As of 2019, before increased federal backing during the COVID-19 pandemic, Americans shouldered more than $25.5 trillion in federal loans, loan guarantees, and subsidized insurance for, among other things, mortgages, deposits, and pensions—provided by close to 150 federal programs.[d] And paying for that burden meant the prospect of huge potential losses.

Housing finance is especially dominated by the federal government. From 2009 to 2020, government-sponsored enterprises Fannie Mae and Freddie Mac's annual share of the total mortgage-backed security (MBS) market averaged 70 percent. Including Ginnie Mae securities, which are backed by Federal Housing Administration mortgages, the federal share of the MBS market averaged 92 percent.[e] Additionally, from 2008 to 2020, the Federal Reserve went from holding zero MBS to holding more than $2 trillion in MBS from Fannie, Freddie, and Ginnie.[f]

Chapter 2

Historical Overview of US Financial Markets

Many Americans are at least vaguely aware that US financial markets are the envy of the world. These markets are the largest, deepest, and most liquid of all, with well-established banking *and* securities segments. Still, relatively few people have more than a superficial knowledge of the history behind US financial markets. Indeed, few have any incentive to look beyond the brief exposure to this history in high school lessons or in the 2015 musical *Hamilton*.

The typical 11th-grade American history text, for example, devotes a few pages to Alexander Hamilton's plan to strengthen America's finances. His plan to solidify the new nation's standing, as many may recall, included creating the Bank of the United States and issuing new federal debt to replace the old Revolutionary War debts. Typically, textbooks also mention that Thomas Jefferson and James Madison opposed Hamilton's plan, favoring a federal government with more limited authority. Jefferson and Madison were bolstered by popular distrust of financial markets. As one text explains, "ordinary Americans" were opposed to Hamilton's plan because "speculators," who had purchased the original war bonds, would "reap a windfall" under the new debt issuance while the "original holders received nothing."[1] The Bank of the United States was ultimately created, but popular distrust of financial markets was not lessened.

Typically, the only other discussion of antebellum American finance in high school history texts involves President Andrew Jackson and his "war" against the Bank of the United States. A passage from one popular text reads:

> The Bank symbolized the hopes and fears inspired by the market revolution. The expansion of banking helped to finance the nation's economic development. But many Americans, including Jackson, distrusted bankers as "nonproducers" who contributed nothing to the nation's wealth but profited from the labor of others.[2]

Super fans of high school history might also remember a brief mention of how Jackson's war against banking helped lead to the Panic of 1837, and how President Martin Van Buren was then left to deal with the resulting depression, which lasted until 1843. But it makes little sense for an introductory American history class to do more than devote a few pages to these events, regardless of how dependent the new nation was on financial markets. There are simply too many details.[3]

Although this book does not attempt to provide a full history of financial markets, it does provide context for the amazing story of American financial markets—a story that is much more complicated than Hamilton versus Jefferson. For starters, this book shows how robust banking and securities markets were from the very Founding of the United States—both on their own terms and compared with financial markets elsewhere.

The extraordinary growth of financial markets was inextricably tied to the new nation's rapid economic growth. Indeed, despite its many deficiencies, America's financial system remains inseparable from America's enormous growth, productivity, and prosperity. Yet for as long as American markets have existed, so has a deeply rooted distrust of these markets.

This distrust has not only long been aimed at "speculators" and "big financiers," it has also heavily influenced the way American financial markets evolved. But make no mistake, despite this deeply rooted distrust, US financial markets are an integral part of what amounts to an economic miracle.

BANKS AND SECURITIES MARKETS WERE—AND STILL ARE—KEY TO AMERICA'S SUCCESS

Immediately after the American Revolution, there was essentially no banking system of any kind, and the US government was in a fiscal mess, with no effective mechanism for levying and collecting taxes to pay its huge debts.[4] Yet by 1792, just four years after the new US Constitution was ratified, newly issued federal debt securities were selling at or above par, a sign that investors believed they would receive what they were promised. Two years later, not only had Congress chartered the Bank of the United States (as promoted by Alexander Hamilton), but 16 state-chartered banks were operating in America. That same year, there were only five incorporated banks, including the Bank of England, in all the British Isles.[5]

By 1801, another 15 state-chartered banks were operating, and 10 of the original states had chartered at least one commercial bank. These banks were not merely empty structures. As economic historian Benjamin Klebaner points out, America's early commercial banks were "the most important and the most successful of the *eighteenth-century* business corporations."[6] By 1840, America had 834 state-chartered banks, and their total (inflation-adjusted) capital had gone from $3 million in 1790 to $4.26 million by 1840, an increase of 42 percent.[7] Between 1820 and 1840, aggregate bank loans went from $55.1 million to $462.9 million, and between 1820 and 1860, bank-supplied credit increased at an annual average rate of 6.3 percent, outpacing the growth of America's aggregate overall economic activity.[8]

One unique feature that helps explain the success of the early American banking system—though it was far from perfect—was that America's banks did not enjoy monopoly privileges as did those in other developed nations at the time. As economic historians Peter Rousseau and Richard Sylla point out:

> From the 1790s to the middle of the 19th century nowhere else in the world was the banking corporation developed as a competitive business enterprise to the extent that it was in the United States.

Only then, six or seven decades after the US innovation, did the older nations of the world begin to emulate the United States by allowing limited liability for banks and other business enterprises.[9]

Thus, competition provided an impetus for these commercial enterprises to help people mobilize their resources, and they were so successful that other countries eventually imitated their methods.

Although the rapid growth in the American banking sector may be well-known to some history buffs, a more obscure fact is that the banking sector developed simultaneously with a rapidly growing *securities* market. In fact, the early American securities market was surprisingly sophisticated. For instance, although the type of structured finance used in the 21st century (to be discussed in chapter 3) was not fully developed until the 1980s, the concepts were in use by the 1780s. Indeed, financial markets during the American *Colonial* period were sophisticated enough to have their own version of asset-backed securities. Colonial governments promoted land banks, which provided mortgages and printed bills backed by those mortgages. These asset-backed bills, in turn, were a liquid security that colonists used as paper money—even to pay taxes.[10]

Obviously, early American securities markets did not closely resemble the fast-paced technology-based trading that is prevalent today. In the 1790s, commercial banks and insurance companies tried to find investors by relying on word of mouth and advertisements in local newspapers. Still, evidence suggests that this method was highly successful, rapidly resulting in millions of dollars being raised.[11] In fact, in 1791, several brokers and auctioneers wrote (and signed) an agreement "with fourteen specific rules" to establish uniform trading procedures. That document was the first step toward formally organizing what in 1792 became the New York Stock Exchange.[12]

In virtually no time, people traded more than just government bonds and private stocks, thereby giving rise to an active securities market. By 1792, investors in the New York market traded various futures and options contracts on the 12 securities that were routinely traded.[13] When prices in the New York market rapidly fell during 1792, the New York legislature made public auctions of securities illegal and outlawed futures and options. Nonetheless, futures, options, and even short sales remained an integral part of the securities market in New York.[14]

These sophisticated markets were not unique to New York. As soon as the young federal government organized and restructured its debt in 1790, organized securities markets also took off in Philadelphia, Boston, and Baltimore. All four markets provided people with regular trading opportunities for government bonds, bank securities, and even securities for local commercial enterprises.[15]

These markets provided asset liquidity to both American and foreign investors, so much so that it helped rapidly overcome investors' hesitancy to hold US debt. In fact, by 1803, at least half the outstanding federal debt, the Bank of the United States' stock, and all US securities issued to that date were held by European investors.[16] The number of listings on these securities markets grew rapidly from 1790 to 1850, with listings for financial institutions increasing particularly fast from 1790 to 1809, and transportation listings increasing rapidly between 1800 and 1809. By 1830, the New York market publicly quoted 75 securities. By 1840, the number was up to 115.[17] By 1850, the markets in Boston, New York, and Philadelphia combined listed nearly 500 securities.[18]

A comparison to England shows that, as of 1825, the number of securities listed in the four major US markets was almost 40 percent of the total number listed in England. Though estimating the *value* of the US equity market in 1825 is not straightforward, one approximation puts the total at $171 million, only a bit less than the total value of the English equity market ($183 million) in 1825.[19] This fact alone is remarkable: less than 30 years from its origin, the American securities market rivaled the largest securities market in the world, one that had had a nearly 100-year head start.

By 1825, the main similarity between England's and America's equity markets was that both listed securities for insurance and transportation companies, as well as for utilities and various manufacturing companies. The main difference, however, was in *banking* securities. Only the American equity market listed numerous bank stocks because, as of 1825, virtually all English banks were either sole proprietorships or partnerships, whereas US banks were limited liability corporations.

Also underappreciated is the cooperative nature of the early American banking and securities markets. That is, the development of the American banking system depended on the development of the securities market and vice versa.[20] Banks raised capital by selling equity securities, and banks' equity securities became more attractive as trading markets developed. As soon as these markets were organized, people could use both government debt and corporate stock as collateral for bank loans, and banks could hold these financial instruments as assets.

This arrangement undoubtedly contributed to the rapid growth of the American financial system. By 1825, though its population was not quite as large as the combined population of Wales and England, the United States had almost 2.5 times the combined banking capital of those two countries.[21] According to economic historian Richard Sylla, by the 1830s there was probably "no place in the world as 'well banked' and 'security marketed' as the northeastern United States."[22] Although the northeastern United States was the hub of the nation's financial markets (and industry), critical systems did develop elsewhere. For instance, by 1840, the banking system in Louisiana accounted for as much as 12 percent of the nation's total banking capital.[23]

Like the financial markets in the Northeast, the financial system in antebellum Louisiana was intimately tied to commerce. In particular, the port of New Orleans, located in the nation's fifth-largest city at the time, handled a large volume of commercial products from all over the Mississippi Valley, much more than agricultural products.[24] Although the securities market in Louisiana did not develop exactly as it did in the northeastern part of the country, financial innovation in Louisiana banks was critical to commercial development. Specifically, these banks engaged in a sophisticated system of deposit credits, a version of what modern economists would call fractional reserve banking. That system depended on widely accepted bank money instead of gold or silver, a critical factor in mitigating the problem of idle—and scarce—capital. Put differently, the system allowed people to leverage the productivity of their existing capital.[25]

Overall, the expansion of financial services in America was also a boon to international trade because the robust financial markets made it easier for merchants to finance shipments and inventories.[26] This process quickly integrated the financial and nonfinancial economies of Great Britain and America, rapidly creating a mature US foreign exchange market. In fact, when previously lost records from the Baltimore foreign exchange, for the period 1791–1829, were discovered in the 1980s, they showed that the foreign exchange market was much more developed than originally thought. The records showed, for instance, that the dollar–sterling exchange rate was much less volatile than other partial records had suggested. Moreover, while older, sparser data suggested that, between 1803 and 1815, the dollar traded below par more than 80 percent of the time, the newly discovered data demonstrated that the dollar traded *above* par more than two-thirds of the time, with an average monthly premium of 3 percent.[27]

Focusing on securities markets and incorporated banks, early American financial markets were undoubtedly sophisticated. The system was even more complex, though, because it included a sizable *private* banking sector as well. Although few historians have provided extensive accounts of the early American private bankers, recent research suggests that this sector was much more important than previously thought. Some even argue that it did not differ significantly from incorporated banks, and renowned historian Bray Hammond states that there were "unauthorized banks everywhere" and notes that "there were also corporations without the name of banks that were engaged in discounting, sale of exchange, and extension of deposit credit."[28]

As with incorporated banks and securities markets, private bankers were not limited to New York. Records indicate, for instance, that private bankers were present in Missouri as early as 1808. Like other private (and incorporated) banks, the Missouri private banks were engaged in taking deposits, paying interest, providing loans, and transmitting funds to most of the main towns and cities in the United States.[29]

Although these banks were formally prohibited from issuing banknotes, they effectively issued currency in the form of bank deposit credits subject to check. (Evidence shows that the use of deposit credit in America is practically as old as America itself.)[30] In fact, during the 1850s, two well-known private banks used this method so successfully that they added approximately 2 percent to the stock of US currency.[31] This type of fractional reserve banking was practiced among both private and incorporated banks. Records for *incorporated* banks show, for example, that during the antebellum period, banks held deposits in excess of the gold and silver (specie) they kept on hand, so a large portion of those deposits must have been either directly or indirectly created.[32]

FINANCIAL MARKET GROWTH CAN'T BE SEPARATED FROM ECONOMIC GROWTH

American financial markets organized in the late 18th century shortly after American independence, developed rapidly, and soon surpassed those of other developed nations. At the same time, the broader American economy grew, rivaling those of the most advanced nations in Europe by the early 19th century.[33] Still, whether the existence of a highly functional financial market caused this economic growth, or whether the nation's rapid commercial development caused financial markets to grow, is difficult to answer empirically.

Evidence suggests, for example, that the largest number of business incorporations took place in the states with the most developed securities markets: New York, Pennsylvania, and Maryland.[34] Similarly, at the very beginning of the 19th century, financial market development in New York was critical to the growth of the nation. Enormous volumes of imports went through New York and on to the rest of the country, and out-of-town merchants could pay for goods using the nascent, but well-developed, New York financial sector.[35] It may be the case that the financial sector jump-started this economic growth; however, it is also plausible that the financial sector developed because of the economic growth occurring at the time.

Economists have studied the relationship between economic growth and financial market development for decades. While there is some disagreement over the direction of the causal relationship, there is no disagreement that financial markets and economic growth are highly connected. Much of the research on the connection between financial markets and economic performance has been done in an international context, where researchers study these relationships in developed countries compared with less-developed countries.

This research is complicated by many technical issues, including how to measure a country's degree of financial market development and the fact that both the amount and quality of economic data vary for many countries. The modern concept of gross domestic product, for example, didn't really exist until the 1900s, so GDP estimates for the early 1800s, for any country, are tenuous at best. Rather than provide a detailed account, this chapter provides only a brief discussion of some relevant empirical findings from this body of literature.

For instance, research suggests that financial frictions—constraints that prevent people from obtaining financing when they need it—help explain much of the observed differences in cross-country per capita output and aggregate productivity.[36] Countries with more financial frictions, interpreted as less developed financial markets, tend to have lower output and productivity. Similarly, a country's level of financial development tends to be positively related to its output per worker. This finding especially holds for one common measure of financial development: the ratio of external finance to GDP, where *external finance* is defined as the sum of private credit plus the capitalization of the private bond and stock markets.[37]

One well-cited 1993 study by Robert G. King of Boston University and Ross Levine of University of California, Berkeley, focuses on the relationship between a country's initial level of financial development and its future rates of *long-run* economic growth. It reports that the initial level of financial development (formally, the "predetermined" component of financial development) is a good predictor of growth over the next 10 to 30 years.[38] The study also reports that higher levels of financial development are "strongly associated with future rates of capital accumulation and future improvements in the efficiency with which economies employ capital."[39]

King and Levine interpret this last finding as evidence that financial market development does not *only* follow commercial economic activity. Sometimes, financial market development comes first, thereby increasing commercial activity. Other researchers have attempted to provide more robust studies of the causality issue. One *American Economic*

Review article, for example, provides both simple correlation and complex causation tests. Using data from the 1980s and 1990s, with a sample of 41 countries, it shows that per capita income is positively correlated to several measures of financial development, including a country's quality of accounting standards and its level of domestic credit as a share of GDP.[40] Figure 2.1 reproduces these results, illustrating that countries with more financial development tend to have higher per capita income.

The same study also undertakes an extensive effort to examine the question of whether financial development causes economic growth, or vice versa. By circumventing several difficulties that previous studies had with this causality issue, the study reports more robust findings that remain consistent with much of the earlier work. That is, these findings suggest, as did many previous studies, that developed financial markets do serve as a catalyst for economic growth. Moreover, these findings also suggest that this catalyst effect is more important for new firms than existing ones.[41]

At the very least, the overall empirical literature is consistent with the idea that a robust financial sector is an essential catalyst for economic growth.[42] Given the core intermediation function

Figure 2.1: Domestic credit ratio by per capita income

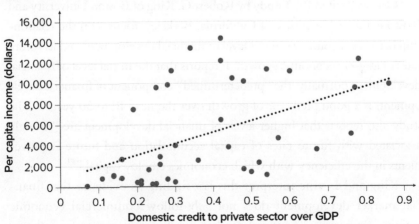

Source: Raghuram G. Rajan and Luigi Zingales, "Financial Dependence and Growth," *American Economic Review* 88, no. 3 (1998): 559–86.

that financial markets serve, channeling capital to where it is most needed, it is difficult to see how financial markets cannot have at least some causal effect on growth. Imagine, for instance, a world where people have no choice other than to bury their savings in their backyard. Then imagine a new law is passed, allowing people to invest their savings in other individuals' businesses, but only on a one-to-one basis. Finally, picture a third phase, in which it becomes legal for people to pool their savings and invest in any financial asset or business. Obviously, there would be more business formation and income opportunities in this third phase because people can more easily direct capital to where it is needed.

Although it may not be so obvious, this third phase is a simplified description of the financial services industry. Both the earliest American financial institutions and modern commercial banks and securities firms serve the same basic function: channeling funds, both directly and indirectly, to the entrepreneurs and business owners who need them.

Incidentally, this basic example also demonstrates why financial markets are often blamed for economic downturns and disasters. Financial markets allow people to take economic risks they otherwise could not have taken, and sometimes those risks do not work out well. And while those underlying risks—a new business venture, an expansion of a factory, and so forth—are often spread throughout the economy, any single financial institution concentrates some of those risks in one place. This kind of risk concentration underscores how important it is for financial institutions to diversify their risks, thus making them more resilient to economic failures so that they can continue to function. When these institutions fail, public distrust of financial markets increases rapidly.

AMERICANS HAVE ALWAYS HAD A LOVE-HATE RELATIONSHIP WITH FINANCE

The distrust that many Americans have long harbored toward financial markets was present at the nation's founding. Indeed, such distrust was on full display during George Washington's inaugural presidency. One faction, led by Thomas Jefferson and James Madison, felt that financial markets mainly benefited "speculators" and "middlemen" at the expense of those who engaged in "real" and "productive" economic activities. The opposing faction, represented by Alexander Hamilton, believed that financial markets were broadly beneficial and critical to unlocking the economic potential of the new nation. The musical *Hamilton*, released in 2015, depicts this battle with Jefferson proclaiming:

> In Virginia, we plant seeds in the ground.
> We create. You just wanna move our money around.
> This financial plan is an outrageous demand,
> and it's too many damn pages for any man to understand.
> Stand with me in the land of the free
> and pray to God we never see Hamilton's candidacy.[43]

This negative view of financial markets cannot be written off as a 21st-century interpretation of an 18th-century political battle; it was evident even in the firsthand accounts of the debate during George Washington's first term as president.[44]

The core of the debate was over how to deal with the new nation's debt, particularly the IOUs the government had issued to conduct the Revolutionary War. Originally, the largest class of these bondholders were soldiers, and the securities were trading on the open market at 20 to 25 percent of their face value.[45] However, as much as 75 percent of the bonds had been sold by their original owners, at a discount, for goods, services, or cash.[46] Thus, the largest class of debt holders after the war were the so-called speculators, not the soldiers who originally held the IOUs. Tellingly, one part of this debate was whether the new government should pay face value to former soldiers who still held the securities, but not to the speculators.

James Madison's mentor, fellow Founder John Witherspoon, argued that the government should not discriminate between the two groups of bondholders. Writing to Hamilton in 1789, he said: "Suppose a clerk in the Bank of England were to tell a person redeeming securities, 'Where did you get these? You are a Speculator . . . we will not pay you the full value of them.' Such a thing reported and believed on the exchange of

London would bring the whole National Debt to the Ground in two Hours."[47] At the time of Witherspoon's letter, Madison had not yet publicly taken a position, but he soon came out in favor of paying the speculators less than face value.[48] Hamilton, on the other hand, strenuously opposed discriminating against the speculators. He recognized that such a scheme would make the bonds worthless on the open market, destroying America's ability to borrow.

Hamilton also displayed a sophisticated understanding of economic uncertainty and subjectivity. He recognized—correctly—that the nation's debts would be worthless if the government discriminated against the speculators, *and* that the speculators' purchases had allowed the original bondholders to immediately meet their needs rather than wait indefinitely. Hamilton also seems to have understood that while the original bondholders paid a price for selling quickly, it would have been impossible for a third party to objectively decide whether that price was the "correct" price. Implicit in Hamilton's argument is the idea that a market price, at any given time, is the most objectively determined price based on the current conditions of the market participants. In his 1790 *Report on Credit*, he wrote:

> How shall it be ascertained, in any [particular] case, that the money which the original holder obtained for his security was not more beneficial to him, than if he had held it to the present time? . . . [And] how shall it be known whether, if the purchaser had employed his money in some other way, he would not be in a better situation . . . though he should now receive the . . . full amount? . . . Questions of this sort, on a close inspection, multiply themselves without end, and demonstrate the injustice of a discrimination, even on the most subtle calculations of equity, abstracted from the obligations of contract.[49]

In his report, Hamilton rebutted several other common fears of the time, some of which remain part of modern discourse. For instance, he argued against the proposition that paying interest to foreign speculators would suck money out of the United States, and the idea that banks benefited only "financial wheeler-dealers."[50] He noted that, instead, what mattered for the good of the nation was the "employment of the capital

by our own citizens."[51] He also rebutted the charge that banks benefited only malicious speculators, arguing that banks "more frequently
enable honest and industrious men, of small, or, perhaps, of no capital,
to undertake and prosecute business."[52]

Firsthand accounts of this period also display some individuals'
love–hate—some might say hypocritical—relationship with finance.
For instance, in his diary, Senator William Maclay from Pennsylvania
decried members of Congress from North Carolina and Connecticut
for speculating in these bonds, and lamented that Hamilton's proposal
would "damn [Hamilton's] character . . . forever."[53] Similarly, Georgia
representative James Jackson criticized the "spirit of havoc, speculation,
and ruin . . . at the avaricious and immoral turpitude which so vile a
conduct displays."[54] Yet both Maclay and Jackson, as many other Americans, were avid speculators in unsettled public lands to the west, much
of which was occupied by Native Americans.[55] In fact, many of those
who speculated in land hedged their positions with the nation's first debt
securities, and vice versa.[56]

This sort of love–hate relationship with financial markets shows
up repeatedly in American history, especially during the economic
difficulties following the Civil War and during the Great Depression.
Moreover, many of these popular attitudes toward financial markets,
especially among the nation's farmers, helped perpetuate the crisis-prone
"unit banking" system, so named because it consisted of small local banks
whose fate was tied to those of local economies.[57] In fact, many historical US political figures are associated with this agrarian populism that
heavily influenced the structure of America's financial markets, including Andrew Jackson and Abraham Lincoln.[58] Broadly, these populists
proclaimed support for the plight of the common man. But while they
displayed a grave mistrust of businesspeople from the cities, especially
bankers, they advocated for wider access to credit so that farmers could
obtain land and equipment.[59] A broad view of the changing economic situation during the 19th century helps explain how and why this
love–hate relationship blossomed.

In the decades before the Civil War, southerners had been almost
entirely reliant on state-chartered banks, all of which were essentially

gone after the war. Even worse for the South, the post–Civil War national banking system required banks to be established with gold and federal government bonds, neither of which existed to any significant extent in the region after the war. As a result, the agricultural system that developed provided farmers with supplies on credit, secured by the future crop yields, typically supplied through a "furnishing merchant" or an "advancing man." This system did not go well for most farmers, and much of the South's farmland was eventually deeded over to these creditors, resulting in former freeholder farmers becoming sharecroppers, who rented the farmland in exchange for a share of the crop going directly to the landlord.[60]

Although the banking system essentially didn't exist for southern farmers throughout much of the postwar period, it was providing credit to the nation's industrial companies and railroads—a situation that farmers viewed as banks' blocking and controlling access to the crucial resources that farmers needed. In the West, more credit was available for land and equipment, but it was typically provided by loan companies that were financed with capital from eastern states, well outside the local regions. As foreclosures on both land and equipment became the norm through the 1890s, westerners' perceived natural enemies became the East Coast financiers and, in a major shift, the gold standard.[61]

Before the war, farmers were among the most ardent supporters of the gold standard and "hard money" because they feared the destruction of purchasing power wrought by inflation from "easy" paper currency. After the Panic of 1873, though, farmers' attitudes shifted because falling commodity prices badly damaged their ability to earn a living. So they primarily feared *deflation* from a money supply that they thought was too "hard." Quite rapidly, farmers began to associate the deflation they were experiencing with the gold standard. Specifically, they saw the deflation as "a consequence of the artificial constraint of the size of the money supply by tethering it to gold."[62] In other words, they now wanted *easy* money precisely because it would lead to inflation and higher commodity prices.

By rejecting the gold standard and calling for the government to increase the money supply, many Americans—not just farmers, but many manufacturers, merchants, and bankers as well—rejected Andrew

Jackson–era policies that explicitly tried to limit the total amount of currency in circulation to guard against inflation.[63] And although those Jackson-era policies had helped drive silver out of circulation before the Civil War, farmers came to view the coinage of silver as an easy way to expand the money supply, thus avoiding the harmful deflation they were experiencing.[64] Formally, they wanted a return to a "bimetallic" standard, in which both gold and silver would serve as the basis for the value of money in circulation.[65]

Despite growing support for a bimetallic standard, the gold standard won a major victory in 1875 when Congress passed the Resumption Act, a law that required the treasury secretary to redeem legal tender paper notes in gold or silver. And although many business owners, including bankers and financiers, soon shifted their support back to maintaining the gold standard, farmers did not. Instead, they became a main force in the "free silver" movement, supporting monetary expansion through the unlimited coinage of silver.[66] Moreover, the farmers supported not just a new form of money, but the public construction of money, with the federal government both defining the money supply and regulating its size.[67] Supporters of the free silver movement came to view the gold standard itself as a harmful policy that favored bankers' interests over those of the common man.[68] They were concerned with who controlled the allocation of money, and they worried that Wall Street financiers had too much control.[69]

It was in this context that, in 1896, William Jennings Bryan gave one of the most famous speeches in American history, his "Cross of Gold" speech, at that year's Democratic National Convention. The speech gave life to bimetallism and the free silver movement, by then a main tenet of the Democratic Party's platform. Bryan told supporters, "In this land of the free you need fear no tyrant who will spring up from among the people."[70] He then called for a president in the mold of Andrew Jackson to take a stand, as Jackson did, "against the encroachments of aggregated wealth."[71] As he ended the speech, Bryan promised that his party would "answer their demands for a gold standard by saying to them, you shall not press down upon the brow of labor this crown of thorns. You shall not crucify mankind upon a cross of gold."[72]

Although Bryan lost the election, his supporters remained a powerful political force into the early 1900s who heavily influenced the legal framework of American financial markets. Their influence, however, was largely a detriment to the welfare of the common man.

Broadly, as more and more corporations merged into giant "trusts" through the 1890s and early 1900s, Bryan's supporters grew increasingly suspicious of large financial companies—derisively known then as the "money trusts"—that operated on Wall Street.[73] The Bryan Democrats saw government control of the issue and size of the money supply as a counter to this supposed force, one that would serve the interests of the common man.[74] Ironically, the policies that the Bryan Democrats favored were often those supported by the "Wall Street" bankers they so detested.

While the Bryan Democrats railed against the Wall Street money trust for controlling their money, the primary driver of the nation's banking structure was quite simple: the post–Civil War era National Banking Act had hard-wired the flow of money from country banks to national banks in New York. Under this legal framework, the smaller (country) banks were required to keep a portion of their reserves at banks in several larger "reserve cities." Those reserve banks, in turn, were required to keep a portion of their reserves in "central" reserve banks in Chicago, St. Louis, and New York. Because money is fungible, some of the reserves in New York banks helped finance activities in New York's securities market. Many people from the interior of the nation viewed this arrangement as "speculation," nothing more than New York financial firms "gambling" with their money.[75] Regardless, this legal framework had created a thriving correspondent banking industry, which allowed banks outside the money centers to hold balances in New York banks, which, in turn, profited by using those funds to make loans.

By 1907, when another major financial panic hit, New York banks held approximately 35 percent of the nation's correspondent balances (equivalent to $500 million), with 80 percent of that total held by New York's six largest banks.[76] As events unfolded in 1907, Bryan argued that the panic itself was part of "the plutocracy's plan to increase its hold upon the government," and that northeastern "big financiers" had caused the currency shortage to "urge the scheme which they have had in mind for years."[77] Bryan and his supporters waged "incessant war" against several reform policies, including one known as "asset currency" that would have allowed banks to issue paper notes backed by their general assets (as opposed to only being able to issue notes backed by government bonds).[78] They viewed asset currency as "part of a conspiracy of major financiers to assert control over the nation's money supply."[79] They also opposed the liberalization of branching restrictions, fearing that branch banking would allow the "money center" banks "to plant their branches in every city or town where they pleased," soon driving "the local institutions out of business."[80]

Ultimately, Bryan's support proved pivotal for the passage of the 1913 Federal Reserve Act.[81] Ironically, the act essentially implemented the same reform plan, embodied in a bill sponsored by Sen. Nelson Aldrich (R–RI), that Bryan and his supporters had worked so hard to defeat.[82] That is, many of the policies that catered to the interests of the Wall Street banks—thus protecting the New York banks' correspondent banking business—made it into the Federal Reserve Act. Rather than move to a system with branch banking and more competitive note issuance, the populists unwittingly helped further entrench the fragile unit banking system.

This fragile unit banking system came almost completely apart during, and likely worsened, the Great Depression. Still, many of these same populist themes surfaced—and even won the day—during the Depression.

A central theme in Franklin Delano Roosevelt's first presidential campaign was that the federal government should act to help struggling people directly and that President Herbert Hoover's approach, instead, had only served to help the "big, monied institutions."[83] For example, in 1933 members of both the Roosevelt administration and Congress derisively labeled the Federal Home Loan Banks as "Hoover creations," accusing them of aiding financial institutions "while doing nothing to help hard-pressed individuals."[84] But the criticisms were not limited to depicting Wall Street institutions as being locked in a zero-sum game with small-town inhabitants. By the time Roosevelt's first term was underway, the idea that speculation had caused the Depression was quite popular.

For instance, the *Yale Law Journal* noted in 1947, "Support for the [securities market] reform program was derived from the widespread belief that the market crash of 1929 was a prime cause of the ensuing depression and the fraud, manipulation and 'excessive' speculation were the basic causes of the market crash."[85] For corroborating evidence, the journal article cites a 1934 Senate hearing report that states, "The fact emerges with increasing clarity that the excessive and unrestrained speculation which dominated the securities markets in recent years, has disrupted the flow of credit, dislocated industry and trade, impeded the flow of interstate commerce, and brought in its train social consequences inimical to the public welfare."[86]

Indeed, this Depression-era "excessive speculation" theme took on a life of its own, and government officials and supposed experts repeated the theme regardless of whether any supporting evidence existed.[87] For instance, on October 3, 1929, UK Chancellor of the Exchequer Philip Snowden described the pre-crash US stock market as a "speculative orgy."[88] Although it is virtually impossible to objectively say whether there was "too much" speculation in the market, contemporaneous reports indicate that there was no hint of major economic weakness leading up to October 1929.[89]

Immediately after the crash, the "excessive speculation" theme spread rapidly, even among well-known economists. Although they should have known better, economists at the time typically failed to specify supporting empirical evidence, and some of them had even taken part in the so-called excessive speculation. Perhaps the best known was none other than John Maynard Keynes, an avid speculator who, after the crash, said, "The extraordinary speculation on Wall Street in past months has driven up the rate of interest to an unprecedented level."[90] Another famous economist, Paul Samuelson, quotes a contemporary of Keynes, P. Sargant Florence, as wryly noting, "Keynes may have made his own fortune and that of King's College, but the investment trust of Keynes and Dennis Robertson managed to lose my fortune in 1929."[91] Thus, before the crash, Keynes was likely betting that stock prices would continue to rise. Chapter 4 further examines the statements of Keynes (and other economists) on financial market speculation, but the key point here is that "excessive speculation" only explains the 1929 crash after the fact (in hindsight).[92] Thus, it isn't much of an explanation at all.[93]

Nonetheless, there is little doubt that this popular view boosted public support for legislation during the Great Depression, with the 1933 Glass-Steagall Act being one of the best-known examples. One of the major changes that Glass-Steagall implemented was federal deposit insurance, a perennial populist policy long supported by small banks and championed by Rep. Henry B. Steagall (D-AL). By one count, between the 1880s and the 1930s, supporters of the unit banking system tried on 150 separate occasions to win federally provided deposit insurance.[94] In 1933, it became a reality when Rep. Steagall agreed to support legislation designed to (among other things) prevent banks from financing stock market speculation, provided the bill was amended to create the Federal Deposit Insurance Corporation.[95] Although Steagall got his wish, the 1933 Glass-Steagall Act became even more famous for legally separating investment banking from commercial banking because of the supposed excesses of Wall Street.

Other than deposit insurance, there are many other examples of populist beliefs influencing the structure of America's financial markets. For instance, in 1933 Congress passed the Home Owners' Loan Act (HOLA), which created federally chartered savings and loan associations (S&Ls, also known as thrifts). At first, the building and loan associations (the local versions of which had existed since the 1830s) opposed these federal charters as damaging to the local nature of their associations, many of which were started by people who did not want to send their money to New York.[96] To pacify the opposition, Section 5 of the HOLA states that the purpose of the new savings and loan associations is to "provide local mutual thrift institutions."[97] For the same reason, the HOLA also confined the bulk of the new S&Ls' lending activity to within 50 miles of each association's home office, and for homes appraised at no more than $20,000.[98]

Thus, the formation of separate categories of financial institutions was largely a response to populist attitudes toward the financial industry.

Both the building and loan industry and its offspring, the savings and loan industry, are two prime examples, but they are not alone. Credit unions, in fact, were a "later expression of the same ideas that guided the historical populists."[99] As Susan Hoffman of Western Michigan University explains, the early proponents of credit unions pushed to create their institutions as part of a "crusade for 'economic democracy.'"[100] In fact, early progressive leaders viewed both credit unions and statutory interest-rate caps for small business loans as fixing the "small loan evil" that they witnessed in the early 20th century.[101] One of the pioneers of the credit union movement in the United States, Roy F. Bergengren, viewed their central purpose as democratizing "control" over resources, touting the benefits of this new institution in which "there is no exterior capital."[102]

Part of the problem with this view, as seen with the fragility of the nation's unit banking system, is that shutting off "exterior capital" is not a winning financial strategy. Moreover, as Hoffman notes, although many populists saw the danger in giving so much control to government officials, the populists believed they could control these dangers by keeping the government "under the control of ordinary people."[103] Regardless of whether this specific populist idea has worked, there is no doubt that a popular anti-finance sentiment has influenced policymakers throughout American history, and it has not always been for the better. At the very least, this sentiment has hindered the kind of informed policy discussions that might foster better financial market policies.[104]

POPULAR FINANCIAL MARKET MYTHS PERSIST

Given the losses and hardship surrounding financial crises, perhaps it is not surprising that so many myths and misunderstandings about financial markets persist. The long-lasting popularity of the Glass–Steagall investment–commercial banking separation, for instance, provides an excellent example of how far a financial crisis can drive a false narrative.[105] In fact, one myth concerning this separation is, essentially, the separation itself. That is, while the Glass–Steagall Act imposed general prohibitions on certain banking and investing activities, it included exceptions in virtually every case, thus falling far short of creating a complete separation of commercial and investment banking.[106] Moreover, virtually no evidence shows that the combination of commercial and investment banking threatened bank safety in the pre–Glass–Steagall era. In fact, much of the evidence supports the opposite conclusion: that the *combination* of investment and commercial banking *strengthened* banks' soundness in the pre–Glass–Steagall era. One of the most—if not the most—meticulous historical accounts of the Glass–Steagall Act, *The Separation of Commercial and Investment Banking* by George J. Benston of Emory University, reports, "The evidence from the pre–Glass–Steagall period is totally inconsistent with the belief that banks' securities activities or investments caused them to fail or caused the financial system to collapse."[107]

Nonetheless, this feature of the 1933 act is still admired by many who believe the legal separation banned the high-risk activities that caused the Great Depression.[108] In fact, the loss of that separation has been widely blamed for the 2008 financial crisis. For instance, one of the demands of the 2011 Occupy Wall Street protestors was to reinstate the Glass–Steagall Act.[109] According to the protestors, as well as elected officials such as Sen. Elizabeth Warren (D-MA), the weakening of those Glass–Steagall restrictions contributed to the 2008 financial crisis.[110] The anger and frustration with the loss and hardship from the Great Depression and the 2008 financial crisis are understandable; however, the evidence does not support that "excessive speculation" caused the Depression. Moreover, there is no reason to believe that a legal separation between commercial and investment banking would have prevented the 2008 crisis.

Another popular myth is that the 2008 crisis was caused by excessive speculation after the financial markets had been deregulated. People regularly blame the 2008 crisis on excessively risky behavior in the so-called shadow banking sector, but the majority of these risky bets—primarily those involving securitized real estate assets—took place in the highly regulated commercial banking sector. That is, it all occurred under the watchful eyes—indeed, with the blessing—of federal banking regulators.[111] For example, the (somewhat exotic sounding) "financial conduits" that were used to issue asset-backed debt were created by *commercial banks* precisely because those banks could provide credit guarantees for the new asset-backed debt securities.[112]

Separately, the (even more exotic sounding) credit default swaps and synthetic collateralized debt obligations made famous by the movie *The Big Short* were launched by employees of J. P. Morgan. At least as far back as 1991, the New York Fed was considering new regulations for these derivative securities. Moreover, the structured investment vehicle concept was pioneered at Citibank.[113] Still, the myth persists that regulators were unaware of these activities because they occurred in the shadows, outside the highly regulated banking sector, a proposition that doesn't hold water. The fact that these kinds of popular myths make it so difficult to have informed policy discussions is unfortunate, especially given the critical functions that financial markets provide. The next chapter provides an overview of these functions, as well as the many different types of financial firms that exist and the many kinds of financial instruments people use.

Chapter 3

Overview of Modern Financial Markets

This chapter demonstrates the enormous depth and breadth of US financial markets. For practically any financing need, people have an abundance of choices. Options for using debt range from simple bank loans to a plethora of short-term debt securities. On the equity side, options range from individual corporate equities to exchange-traded funds. Hedge funds and private equity firms use all kinds of instruments to help thousands of companies raise capital, and people can choose from a wealth of derivative securities to guard against specific financial risks. As people trade these financial assets, money flows through thousands of financial institutions.

Ultimately, these markets help people direct scarce resources—including capital—to their most productive uses. Without such robust financial markets, obtaining the goods and services that improve living standards would be much more difficult and expensive. Still, the abundance of choices makes US financial markets ripe for criticism, especially from those who fear "excessive speculation."[114] And investors have so many different options that it is easy to criticize people for simply "speculating" rather than investing in "real" goods. As discussed in chapter 2, even critics in 18th- and 19th-century America cast "speculators" and "nonproducers" as exploitative and wasteful, arguing that they sought to profit off others' productive efforts while contributing nothing "real" to the nation's wealth.

Financial market critics have refined this theme over time, but it remains largely the same. For instance, in the 1960s, 1970s, and 1980s, several socialist critics of the American economy, such as Paul A. Baran, Paul Sweezy, and Harry Magdoff, argued that the growth of financial activity and speculation had contributed to economic stagnation.[115] Critics on the American right have made similar arguments: sticking with the stagnation theme, Senator Marco Rubio (R–FL) released a report in 2019 on domestic business investment, arguing, "For the first time, the nonfinancial corporate business sector now consistently spends more on acquiring financial assets than on capital development."[116] This language is just the "wasteful nonproducers" theme cloaked in newer economic terminology. But the core idea remains the same: speculation on financial items is viewed as wasteful, whereas speculation on productive (real, or capital) goods is beneficial.

Some critics, such as Rubio, go even further, distinguishing between "good" and "bad" types of economic growth fueled by financial markets. For instance, Rubio's report claims, "Economic growth is now more driven by finance than innovation in the production of real assets."[117] Thus, while such critics acknowledge that financial market activity contributes to economic growth, they claim that this type of growth is harmful unless it comes from directly investing in capital development. But this refinement only magnifies the major flaws contained in the original "wasteful nonproducers" view.

From the beginning, a major flaw in this critique has been that there is no objective way to distinguish "good" from "bad" speculation. All investments are speculative, and even those that do not raise money for capital goods indirectly affect capital development. In the extreme, banning investments that do not directly raise money for capital development would make capital goods scarcer, leaving people less productive and with a lower standard of living. As discussed in chapter 2, a less extreme example of this phenomenon occurred in the late 18th century, when some members of Congress wanted to pay so-called speculators in government bonds less than they were owed.

Not only is the "wasteful nonproducers" view misguided in theory, but it is dangerous in practice because it implies that policies should be implemented to reduce the number of financial assets. Such a reduction would be problematic because a more limited financial market, one with a smaller number of financial assets and fewer types of assets, is more fragile.[118] Such a policy is the opposite of one that would maximize the opportunity for the largest number of people to adequately diversify their assets and build the most wealth as safely as possible. Allowing people to create the broadest possible set of assets is the surest way to develop resilient financial markets.

The implications of this view are even more dangerous for modern American securities markets. As this chapter explains, none of the trading that occurs on secondary markets—stocks traded through an E*Trade account, or on the New York Stock Exchange, for example—does anything to directly raise capital. Yet secondary market trades indirectly affect the ability of people to raise capital, just as the trades of the so-called speculators during the early days of the republic indirectly affected the government's ability to raise money. Put simply, if millions of people will regularly pay for securities, then companies can more easily sell shares to raise capital.

Moreover, restricting financial market activity in this manner requires giving someone the authority to dictate what the value should be for all sorts of goods and services *and* to stop people from investing in anything deemed to be of insufficient value. This is anathema to a market mechanism for determining what is valuable.

Unsurprisingly, critics deride the role of the market in determining value. For instance, Rubio's investment report laments: "Decisions about ultimate value must be decided somewhere, or by someone. In the U.S., we have outsourced these decisions so fully to mere market preference that we have made it easy to deny that a decision must be made at all."[119] Yet allowing "market preference" to decide ultimate value merely means that millions of people are deciding what is most valuable to them. Outsourcing decisions over how to allocate capital to "market preference" is not turning the decisionmaking power over to someone. Rather, it allows millions of people to "vote" on how to allocate capital by choosing what to do with their money.

Advocates of proposals such as Rubio's reject what people view as valuable and beneficial, insisting that only a select few—perhaps members of Congress or regulators—know what is truly valuable and best for everyone. Such proposals would empower this group—not the millions of people earning money and investing it—to decide what everyone can do with their money.

As discussed in chapter 5, a great deal of financial regulation already functions in this manner, such that federal regulators decide what people may or may not do with their own money. To provide better context for this discussion, the present chapter provides an overview of the main functions financial markets serve. It also provides an overview of the main types of financial firms and the main types of financial instruments these firms use.

FINANCIAL MARKETS SERVE VITAL FUNCTIONS

As with all types of companies, technology has changed the way financial firms operate, especially over the past two centuries. And although more types of financial companies now provide more financial services to a broader group of customers, the main functions that financial markets serve are largely the same as they have always been. Many of the details have changed; however, the main reasons financial markets exist have not.

The most important function financial markets serve is to help people allocate capital in the most productive way possible. To do this, many financial firms serve as financial intermediaries between people who want to provide funds to others and those who need additional funds. Commercial banks and investment banks are intermediaries that allocate capital directly. They pool individuals' funds and channel those funds to other people and businesses that need capital.

Although not all financial firms allocate capital *directly*—firms that facilitate secondary-market transactions of financial instruments, for example—financial market activities improve capital allocation at least indirectly. And these functions are not always discrete, as the following summary shows. Many financial firms serve multiple functions, many of which reinforce each other.[120]

- *Discover prices.* Financial markets promote price discovery for assets by allowing large numbers of people to use their own money to weigh in on what they believe the assets are worth. In any market, when buyers and sellers interact, they must agree on a price to make a transaction. Financial markets are where supply and demand meet to arrive at an asset price at which most participants are willing to buy and sell. The more buyers and sellers for a given asset, the better the asset's price will reflect what most people believe the asset is worth. That price can change—sometimes rapidly—as buyers and sellers incorporate new information into their decisions to buy or sell.
- *Provide liquidity.* Liquidity refers to the ease with which an asset can be sold with little loss of its value. When assets can be sold very quickly with virtually no loss of their value, they are said to be highly liquid. Cash and US government bonds tend to be very liquid, whereas assets such as houses and land are less liquid. Various financial firms provide liquidity by connecting buyers and sellers on a regular basis. People often place a premium on liquidity for two major reasons. First, liquidity provides flexibility and the opportunity to move into other assets quickly. Being able to quickly move out of one investment to another, without substantial loss of value, allows people to respond to unexpected events or emergencies more easily without damaging their ability to earn or produce over the long term. Second, it allows people to change their mind about their risk tolerance or about the value of a project their capital is funding, with minimal costs.
- *Mitigate risks.* Robust financial markets help people reduce many types of risks. For instance, they allow people to diversify their investment risk by making it easier to buy assets with unrelated risk characteristics. Because the returns

of such assets are not perfectly correlated—they do not move in the same direction, at the same rate—diversified investors can eliminate some of the risk of their overall return being less than expected from discreet investments. As a result, financial firms that help people diversify provide lower liquidity risk and price risk. Financial firms also lower individuals' risk by being able to better accept maturity mismatches that arise from holding long-term assets while having short-term liabilities. Derivatives markets—which specialize in assets whose value is derived from some other asset—even allow people to protect themselves against certain risks without purchasing the underlying assets causing those risks. Robust financial markets also allow individuals to purchase insurance against losses from adverse events, including the loss of life and property.

- *Reduce information, monitoring, and transaction costs.* Financial firms can collect and produce information at a lower average cost than individual investors can. These firms can, for example, conduct extensive research on thousands of companies. Such information can then be more easily passed on to individual investors. Firms providing such information services have a greater incentive than any individual investor both to collect more information and to monitor and report on the performance of the companies in an investment fund's portfolio. Thus, financial firms can lower investors' information, monitoring, and transaction costs by pooling funds from many people. It is more cost-effective, for instance, to spread fees across thousands of investors than for those thousands of investors to incur the same expenses individually, because a large financial institution will have a lower average cost of both trading and of collecting and using information than an individual investor would.

- *Smooth consumption.* When consumers take on debt, it allows them to purchase goods and services immediately rather than wait until the future. Instead of consuming more later in life, when they earn more income or have more savings, people can spread their purchases out more evenly over time, consuming more now than they would be able to without incurring debt. That is, debt allows people to smooth their lifetime consumption pattern. The same principle applies to firms. When people organize businesses, financial markets help them spread their business's costs out over many years, thus making it easier to access more capital and grow their operations.

- *Provide payment services.* Robust financial markets also help provide payment services that make it easier for people to buy and sell all kinds of goods and services by transferring money easily and quickly. Simply put, they help people pay for consumer goods and services as well as buy and sell assets.

Combined, these features help explain how and why robust financial markets assist people in creating wealth.

First, the core function of capital allocation helps people be more productive. As people become more productive—as they put physical capital to better use—they produce more goods and services with less labor. Thus, this first function alone helps improve people's lives both directly and indirectly, through a higher standard of living and new opportunities to earn income and save labor.

Second, by lowering transaction and monitoring costs, financial firms provide broader access to investments and ownership in companies, even for people who do not already have large amounts of wealth or a high income. Robust financial markets, along with basic technological innovations, now provide virtually all Americans with low-cost access to many different kinds of investments, either directly or indirectly through investing in funds. This access allows more people than ever to share in the profits of even the largest corporations of the world with relatively small investments.

Because they provide liquidity, financial markets also mitigate the risks of investing in long-term assets. In the absence of broad liquidity, many people would rather hold on to their cash than invest, for example, in a business. Financial markets help alleviate this type of incentive problem because liquidity creates the expectation of being able to easily convert an investment to cash. This flexibility helps promote capital allocation and price discovery, and helps people diversify and lower their investment risks. It does so *broadly* because the larger, more diverse, and more liquid markets become, the more opportunities exist for making new investments.

FINANCIAL FIRMS OPERATE IN MULTIPLE SEGMENTS

As would be expected in any well-developed market, many different types of financial firms operate in America. Many financial firms specialize in providing a limited number of services, or in using specific financial instruments; however, types of financial activities frequently overlap, and often reinforce each other.

To better describe what financial firms do, it helps to classify financial activities into various groupings. Not all firms fall neatly into these categories, but many of the individual services they provide tend to fall into one or the other.

The most common distinction is between banks and nonbank financial firms. Although the line is blurry, banks have traditionally been focused on providing deposit services and loans, whereas nonbank financial firms have provided a much wider array of financial services.

On the nonbank side, it is common to distinguish between financial activities that occur in primary markets and those that occur in secondary markets.

Primary markets are where people raise money that goes directly into funding a business. For example, when Apple issues new shares of stock, anyone who purchases those shares *directly* funds Apple's operations. The money goes to Apple, and Apple can use it to build a new headquarters, to purchase equipment, or to pay employees. Primary markets can be thought of as a new-car market, where the buyers' money goes straight to the manufacturer, through the dealership.

Secondary markets, on the other hand, are where people purchase assets that were previously sold in the primary markets. When shares are purchased on secondary markets, the money used for those purchases does not go to the company that issued the shares. The money used on the secondary market to purchase shares of Apple, for instance, does not go to Apple. Instead, the money goes to the current owner of those shares, who may or may not be the same person who originally bought the shares on the primary market. Secondary markets can be thought of as a used-car market, where buyers' money goes to a previous owner rather than to the manufacturer.

Although secondary-market purchases do not directly provide issuing firms with capital, these purchases still provide benefits to the companies that issue securities. Most importantly, they enhance liquidity and price discovery. Companies that issue securities in the primary market learn how investors perceive the value of their company, which provides a sort of testimony on how well companies are using the funds they've raised in the primary market, and on how much they could raise if they chose to raise more money in the primary market.

Because liquidity refers to how easily someone can sell a security without loss of value, having a highly liquid secondary market provides benefits as well. Not only does it provide rapidly updated pricing information, but it makes it easier for firms to issue new securities in the primary market. That is, liquid secondary markets enhance the ability of firms—both new and old—to raise money directly from investors. Naturally, these benefits help improve the allocation of capital, making it easier for companies to provide goods and services in a more productive fashion, thereby improving people's living standards over the long term.

Another common distinction among nonbank financial firms is between activities that occur in capital markets and those that occur in money markets. The key determinant between these types of markets is the term to maturity—the time component—of an asset. In money markets, people trade many types of short-term debt instruments, which mature in one year or less. Money markets consist largely of people who want to lend funds for only a short time and those who need to borrow for only a short time.

Conversely, in capital markets, people trade assets with maturities of more than one year. In many cases, these assets have no definite maturity at all. A share of stock, for instance, has no maturity because it doesn't "expire." It can be held indefinitely, and it can even be passed on from one generation of owners to another. Stocks and long-term debt instruments are good examples of assets that trade in capital markets.

Well-developed financial markets consist of robust primary *and* secondary markets, with an abundance of instruments trading in both money markets and capital markets. Still, these designations are not inclusive. Derivatives markets, for instance, are more difficult to classify because, among other reasons, the value of derivative securities is tied to—derived from—the value of other assets. For instance, a manufacturer might purchase a derivative security to protect itself if the price of steel were to rise in two years. The price of such a derivative would depend on, among other things, the current price of steel and the expected future price of steel. Similarly, an airline—or a catering company that sells to an airline—might purchase derivatives to protect itself against an increase in the price of jet fuel.[121]

Although derivatives have a (somewhat deserved) reputation for being risky, they have proved themselves to perform valuable functions in well-developed financial markets. Many financial and *nonfinancial* firms use derivatives, as well as more standard money market and capital market instruments, to fund their operations and manage financial risk. As the next section demonstrates, there are many different types of financial firms and financial instruments.

MAJOR TYPES OF FINANCIAL INSTITUTIONS AND INSTRUMENTS

As mentioned earlier, all kinds of firms provide financial services. Many of these financial institutions focus only on money markets, capital markets, primary markets, or secondary markets. Still, some financial firms operate in some combination of these different categories. The following list provides an overview of the major types of financial institutions and the main types of financial instruments they provide. Some firms, of course, provide more than one type of instrument or, at the very least, some type of service related to multiple instruments.

FINANCIAL INSTITUTIONS

COMMERCIAL BANKS

The core function of commercial banks is to accept customers' deposits and use those funds to provide loans to individuals and businesses. They function as intermediaries that directly allocate capital—that is, they use customers' deposits to fund loans. Most people view their bank as a place to store their money, but that view is not completely accurate. While banks must return their customers' deposits on demand, banks use deposited funds to finance business investments and consumer purchases. Thus, when they lend, banks also create deposits—this time by the borrowers.

Banks' customers, in the aggregate, always have some money on deposit, so banks lend a portion of the money on deposit to borrowers. Because banks are always obligated to make customers' account balances available for withdrawal, many people criticize this method of lending, known as fractional reserve banking, as overly risky.[122] Although such critics call for requiring full reserves—rather than reserves for a portion (a fraction) of the amount of outstanding loans—moving to such a model would either reduce the amount of lending in an economy or drive that lending activity to other types of financial intermediaries. Requiring full reserves would make it more expensive to provide credit, thereby reducing the total amount available in the economy. Thus, to the extent that it does not reduce economic activity altogether, requiring full reserves in the banking sector would merely move economic risks to other types of financial firms.

While different banks specialize in different types of loans, commercial banks generally make personal, commercial, and industrial loans. Some businesses, for instance, use commercial loans to finance their inventory and computer and other equipment purchases, whereas other companies use industrial loans to fund new buildings, storage facilities, or manufacturing plants.

Because all banks must make funds available to their deposit customers on demand, even when they have used those funds to make a loan to a borrower, they tend to prefer making shorter-term loans (no longer than five years). Banks also use deposited funds to buy other financial instruments, such as municipal bonds, Treasury bills, and mortgage-backed securities. Many of these financial instruments, especially Treasuries, are highly liquid so that the bank can sell them quickly to provide its customers' deposits on demand.

As of June 2023, there were 4,645 federally insured banks in the United States, with domestic deposits of $17.2 trillion.[123] Against these deposits, the banks made $12.3 trillion in loans.

SAVINGS INSTITUTIONS

Savings associations, thrifts, savings banks, and credit unions all perform functions similar to those provided by commercial banks. These institutions tend to concentrate on one segment of the market, such as real estate or agriculture; however, they typically provide loans to all types of customers.[124] As of June 2023, there were 574 federally insured savings institutions in the United States, with domestic deposits of $1.02 trillion.[125] In the fourth quarter of 2022, there were 4,760 federally insured credit unions, with $1.8 trillion in deposits and $1.5 trillion in outstanding loans.[126]

INSURANCE COMPANIES

Various types of insurance companies protect individuals and businesses from the financial consequences of adverse events. Life insurance companies, for example, protect people against financial losses associated with untimely illness or death, as well as loss of regular income when they retire. Property and casualty insurance companies, on the other hand, protect against losses from personal injury, automobile accidents, storms, fires, and so forth. Consumers pay insurance companies premiums, which the companies invest to settle future claims. Although insurance companies mainly serve to mitigate risk, they are also financial intermediaries, selling products such as variable life insurance and annuities that serve as investment vehicles for some people.[127]

Within the insurance sector, life insurance companies play the largest role in financial intermediation. As of the end of 2021, there were 737 life insurance companies in the United States with $8.7 trillion in assets.[128]

Still, virtually all types of insurers participate in some form of financial intermediation with the insurance premiums they collect. Broadly, along with pension funds and other investment companies, insurance companies fall into a class of investors known as *institutional* investors, identified as institutions that pool large sums of money to make large investments. For example, as of the end of 2022, life insurance companies had invested $3.6 trillion in bonds, $210 billion in equity securities, and $695 billion in mortgages, and US property and casualty insurers separately invested $1.2 trillion in bonds and $817 billion in equity securities.[129]

INVESTMENT BANKS

An investment bank does not take deposits like a commercial bank does, but rather it functions as an intermediary that provides financial services related to financial transactions. Although investment banking and commercial banking have been required to maintain some degree of separation, both under the Glass-Steagall Act and after it was amended in 1999, many of the most recognizable financial services brands—Citigroup, Bank of America, JPMorganChase, and Goldman Sachs, for example—engage in both investment and commercial banking.

Investment banks serve varied and diverse functions, and each bank may specialize in providing a different set of services. In fact, investment banks are often characterized as being either "buy side" or "sell side," meaning that some banks focus on providing advice to institutions that *buy* investment services, whereas others focus on providing services related to *selling* (i.e., trading or promoting) securities.

In general, investment banks underwrite and advise companies seeking to issue securities, such as in an initial public offering, but they also advise on other transactions, such as mergers and acquisitions. Investment banks provide other financial advisory services, such as financial advising or brokerage services for clients, most often institutional clients or high-net-worth individuals. They provide research on companies, giving advice on the desirability of investing in a particular company. Some investment banks sponsor investment funds. Investment banks also often engage in proprietary trading—in other words, trading on their own account, not on behalf of a customer.

Counting investment banks can be challenging because of the diverse nature of their businesses—and because investment banks are not regulated as "investment banks" per se, but rather by the function they are performing. Some estimates place the number of investment banks in the United States at around 3,000, with about a dozen large banks—known as "bulge bracket" banks—that handle the largest transactions and the largest clients.[130] Investment banking revenue in the United States in 2023 was estimated at approximately $32 billion.[131]

Investment banks can be regulated as broker-dealers, investment advisers, or both.

BROKER-DEALERS

Brokers buy or sell securities on the account of other parties, and dealers buy or sell securities on their own account.[132] Although it is possible for an organization to be just a broker or just a dealer, most engage in both activities. Broker-dealers are financial intermediaries that provide investment advice to customers, facilitate trading activities, and create liquidity in markets, both by matching buyers and sellers and by buying and selling themselves. Broker-dealers are generally compensated by the transaction, rather than by taking an ongoing fee for money that is invested.

Broker-dealers have roles in both the primary and secondary securities markets. Only some broker-dealers are involved in the primary market, helping to distribute newly issued securities and to directly raise capital for companies. In this capacity, broker-dealers assist companies in preparing their securities offerings. Specifically, they assess the market interest in an offering, set the initial price for the offering, and sell the security to investors.[133] Other broker-dealers are involved in the secondary market, where investors sell previously issued securities to other investors. Broker-dealers also run the gamut from large financial institutions that sell their own financial products to independent companies that facilitate trading in products offered by others to fully online brokerages that provide trading platforms to customers. Broker-dealers can be what is known as "full-service," which means they provide a large variety of financial services to customers, including tax planning or investment research, or "discount," which specialize in executing customers' trades.

In 2022, 3,378 broker-dealers were registered with the Financial Industry Regulatory Authority (FINRA), the self-regulatory organization that oversees the industry.[134] More than 620,000 individuals worked for these broker-dealers.[135] The total number of brokerage firms has been declining in recent years, as has the total number of individuals registered with FINRA (although 2022 saw an uptick in the number of registered representatives).[136] Rather than clearly showing a shrinking industry, these trend lines show a combination of firm consolidation as well as a shift from individuals registered as brokers to individuals functioning as investment advisers.[137]

INVESTMENT ADVISERS

Investment advisers are individuals or companies that are paid for providing their clients advice about securities. These advisers are known by several names, including asset managers, portfolio managers, and wealth managers. Investment advisers can be regulated by the Securities and Exchange Commission (SEC) or by state securities regulators, depending on the amount of assets that the adviser is managing. Investment advisers with more than $100 million under management must register with the SEC.

Investment advisers do not, themselves, execute securities transactions. To implement the advice they provide to their clients, they have to use other securities professionals, such as broker-dealers. It is common for investment advisers to be dually registered as broker-dealers as well, so one individual could provide multiple services in some cases.[138]

Investment advisers serve many roles. Some provide personalized investment advice to individual clients, whereas others manage investment portfolios for institutional clients or investment funds.[139] Advisers also increasingly use digital platforms to provide investment advice. They are typically compensated by either a fee for service or an ongoing percentage of the assets they are managing. Advisers have a fiduciary duty to their clients, which generally requires them to put their clients' best interests before their own.

In 2022, there were more than 30,000 investment adviser firms in the United States.[140] Approximately half of those firms are registered with the SEC, and they employ the vast majority of investment adviser representatives.[141] Still, most investment advisers are small businesses—over half of the advisers have only one office, with the median adviser employing only eight people.[142]

This industry has seen steady growth over the past two decades.[143] At the end of 2022, more than $114 trillion in assets were managed by SEC-registered investment advisers, serving almost 62 million clients.[144]

INVESTMENT COMPANIES

An investment company is a company that issues securities and is primarily engaged in the business of investing in securities.[145] Investment companies invest the money they receive from investors, and each investor shares in the profits and losses in proportion to the investor's interest in the company. The exact design of the investment company can vary, affecting the way in which investors can purchase and redeem their shares in the company, as well as the structure of the company's investments. Investment companies are divided by the securities laws into three types: mutual funds, closed-end funds, and unit investment trusts. They are required to register with the SEC, although some investment funds—like hedge funds or private equity funds—are exempted from such registration because they limit the number or type of their investors and thus are not classified as "investment companies."

Investment companies straddle the line between being financial institutions and financial products themselves. That is, investment companies themselves are a type of financial company that intermediates the investments of a pool of investors. Yet these investors view the investment company—the mutual fund, for example—as a financial instrument. For this reason, the most popular investment company types will be described next as financial instruments.

FINANCIAL INSTRUMENTS

STOCKS

Stocks, also known as equity securities, represent the ownership of a fraction of the issuing corporation and entitle the stock's owner to a portion of the company's assets and profits. Beyond this basic concept, the form of company stock has many variations. Owning stock may give an investor the right to participate in the management of the company by voting in shareholder meetings, and it may give the shareholder the right to receive distributions from the company, such as dividend payments. But not all stocks provide the same shareholder rights or entitlement to distributions, and some companies issue multiple classes of shares that have different rights.

Stocks are issued by companies to raise capital, and in return for that capital, the shareholder is entitled to a portion of the company's assets and profits. This capital raising happens when the share is issued for the first time. When a company issues shares to the public for the first time, it is known as an initial public offering (IPO). Still, issuances of new shares of equity happen at many stages in a company's life cycle, including by privately held companies and by older publicly traded companies issuing new shares. After that initial issuance, the shares trade in what is known as the secondary market, where money is exchanged between the holder of the security and its buyer.

Public company stocks are traded on stock exchanges, such as the New York Stock Exchange or NASDAQ. The number of companies listed on stock exchanges has been declining since the 1990s, with a total of 4,266 in 2019 down from over 8,000 at the peak.[146] Estimates in 2023 place that total number even lower, at approximately 3,700.[147] The number of IPOs have correspondingly declined from highs in the 1990s, with only 54 IPOs taking place in 2023.[148]

Other stocks, including of companies that have made public offers of securities, are traded in what is known as the over-the-counter (OTC) market, where trading is facilitated on a one-to-one basis with a broker or dealer.[149] Some company stock, particularly stock in privately held companies, is restricted, which means that it cannot be traded unless certain conditions are met.

US equities markets have a $40.3 trillion market capitalization—in other words, the total value of the stock traded is $40.3 trillion.[150] This amount represents about 40 percent of the global total, and US markets are more than 3.5 times the size of the next-largest market, China.[151] US markets are not only the largest in the world, they are also the most liquid, with an average trading volume in 2022 of 11.9 billion shares, constituting $573 billion in value exchanging hands daily.[152]

These markets are used by both institutional investors and individual investors. As of 2022, 58 percent of American households held stock, an all-time high, and that percentage has been growing over time.[153] US households held $39.7 trillion of equities in 2022 (directly and indirectly through funds).[154] US households directly held 41 percent of US equities and institutional investors held the remaining 59 percent of equities, including equities indirectly held by households through their retirement funds, among other assets.[155]

BONDS

Bonds, also known as fixed-income or debt securities, represent a loan made by an investor to a borrower and the borrower's agreement to pay periodic interest and repay the principal. Bonds have a maturity date—when principal is due to be paid back to the investor—and the interest that is paid during the life of the bond is set by the terms of the loan. Bonds can be issued by a corporation or by a government entity.

Because the principal is to be paid back at maturity and the investor is entitled to a predicable income stream while holding the bond, bonds are usually viewed as a less risky investment than equities. Bonds are not without risk, however: one large risk that an investor must consider is whether the borrower will be able to make interest payments or repay the principal when the bond matures. That risk varies with the issuer, of course. US Treasury bonds are generally viewed as low risk because the US government is unlikely to default, whereas so-called junk bonds—on which the issuer is likely to default—are viewed as high-risk investments. Bonds are also subject to interest rate and inflation risk, both of which affect the attractiveness of the bond to both the issuer and investor.

Like other securities, including equities, new—or primary—bond issuances give capital directly to the issuer. Additionally, trading between investors occurs on the secondary market, where individuals buy and sell bonds. Unlike equities, however, few bonds trade on exchanges. Most bonds are traded in the over-the-counter market.[156] One of the main reasons for this mode of trading is that bonds, especially corporate bonds, can be quite diverse. The same issuer can have many different bonds outstanding at the same time, with different maturities, different interest arrangements, and different principals, and each having a different credit rating. Over-the-counter trading tends to be less regulated, less transparent, and less liquid than exchange trading. Whereas markets for US Treasuries are highly liquid, corporate bond markets can be highly illiquid, with few buyers and sellers transacting in any particular bond.[157]

The bond markets are larger than equities markets but are more heavily skewed toward institutional investors. In 2022, US fixed-income markets comprised $51.9 trillion of outstanding securities, or approximately 40 percent of the global total.[158] Corporate bond issuances exceed equity issuances: for example, in 2022, $1.35 trillion of corporate debt was issued, compared with $99 billion in equity.[159] However, as of June 2022, only 3 percent of US household investable assets were held in bonds, as opposed to 23 percent held directly in stocks.[160]

COMMERCIAL PAPER

Commercial paper is a short-term debt instrument that firms—both financial and nonfinancial—issue to finance their short-term needs, such as payroll, receivables, and inventory. The US commercial paper market has existed since the early 19th century and has consistently worked as a source of short-term nonbank credit—working capital—for large companies.[161]

Most commercial paper is issued only by very large corporations with stellar credit ratings, such as Ford, John Deere, and Citigroup.[162] It is issued in large denominations (at least $100,000), and it matures on a specific date. Although the term can be as much as 270 days, most commercial paper matures in less than one week.[163] Generally, only large institutional investors—such as private pension funds, commercial and investment banks, and mutual funds—can buy commercial paper, so most retail consumers only have access to these investments through specialized funds, such as a money market mutual fund.

When they buy commercial paper, institutional investors lend money to commercial companies, providing them with cash for a short period. Many of those institutional investors have a cash surplus, and many commercial firms need extra cash, so the commercial paper market serves as a low-cost alternative to a bank loan. Typically, commercial paper is issued at a discount from face value, meaning that a buyer pays less than face value and then receives the full face value at maturity; the difference is the buyer's profit.

The commercial paper market is highly liquid, with very short-term maturities, so it is common for issuers to *roll over* their commercial paper, meaning that they constantly issue new paper—borrow more—to pay off their maturing issues.

Traditionally, commercial paper was unsecured debt, but *asset-backed* commercial paper (ABCP) is secured debt. It is usually issued by commercial banks and typically backed by specific assets—such as auto loans, home mortgages, credit card debt, or some combination of those—that serve as collateral. Though ABCP has generally been more expensive than traditional commercial paper, companies use both types as a low-cost alternative to bank debt. Normally, commercial banks set up special entities, known as conduits, to issue ABCP and provide credit or liquidity guarantees. In other words, most asset-backed commercial paper is sold with explicit guarantees that require commercial banks to pay full face value in the event of default.[164]

As of December 2023, total US commercial paper outstanding was $1.2 trillion, roughly half as much as the all-time high, which was reached in July 2007.[165] For comparison, total outstanding US commercial/industrial bank loans amounted to $2.8 trillion.[166]

REPURCHASE AGREEMENTS

Repo agreements have existed in the United States since at least 1917, when the Federal Reserve used them to extend credit to member banks.[167] The repo market is sort of a commercial paper market for financial institutions—the Fed's primary dealers, banks, insurance companies, and pension funds are among the largest participants.[168] And although the Fed remains heavily involved in the repo market, securities dealers rely heavily on repos to provide liquidity in money markets, especially the secondary market for US Treasuries. For more than a decade, the average daily outstanding repo balance has been approximately $4 trillion.[169]

Repos are debt instruments by which one party agrees to sell securities—often Treasury securities—for cash *and* to repurchase those same securities later (usually the next day) at a higher price.[170] Thus, a repo agreement is a type of short-term debt. Specifically, it is a collateralized short-term loan in which one party borrows cash from another and provides securities for collateral.

If the borrower fails to repurchase the securities as promised, the lender keeps the securities. Generally, the borrower overcollateralizes the loan by borrowing less than the value of the securities. By posting, for example, $1 million in Treasuries as collateral, a firm could borrow $985,000. The Federal Reserve has engaged in repo transactions since its inception, mainly as a lender of cash to its primary dealers in the conduct of its normal monetary policy—open market—operations. Starting in 2013, however, the Fed has also been a borrower in the repo market, using its Overnight Reverse Repurchase Program to allow primary dealers and other financial institutions, including mutual funds, to deposit cash at the Fed overnight in return for borrowing the Fed's securities.[171]

Repos allow firms with large pools of cash to earn interest on their funds while providing borrowers with an inexpensive, low-risk alternative to bank loans for short-term financing. They can be for terms of up to two years, but most repos are issued on an overnight basis.[172] US Treasury securities are by far the most commonly used collateral in the repo market, with agency debt and agency mortgage-backed securities a close second, such that approximately 70 percent of the collateral used in the repo market consists of government-backed securities.[173]

As with commercial paper, it is common for issuers to roll over their borrowings, meaning that they constantly issue new repos to pay off maturing issues. The denominations are typically very large—in the millions of dollars—so only large firms are involved in the repo market.[174] Historically, securities dealers have been the largest borrowers in the repo markets, with an average share of more than 53 percent of total borrowings for the past two decades. They also have been the largest *investors* in the repo market, accounting for 40 percent of the total share for the past 20 years.[175] In other words, securities dealers usually exchange both cash and securities in the repo market for their clients, so much so that the dealers are the largest participants in both sides of the market.[176]

ASSET-BACKED SECURITIES

Although it can be complex and detailed, the securitization of assets involves nothing more than forming groups—pools—of assets, such as mortgages, consumer loans, or other financial assets, and then creating securities tied to those assets. The process is used to create, for example, mortgage–backed securities and asset–backed commercial paper, as well as lesser-known securities backed by auto loans and credit card receivables. The general idea is that by aggregating multiple financial assets and packaging them into different securities with distinct maturities and risk characteristics, they will appeal to a wide array of investors with diverse needs. Some securities are designed to be very low risk, whereas others are not. Before the 1980s, securitization was essentially only done using mortgages for the underlying assets, largely through the government-sponsored enterprise (GSE) Fannie Mae. Then in 1985, Sperry Corporation sold $200 million in securities backed by a pool of leases on computer equipment, essentially opening a floodgate of new securitizations.[177]

After that sale, financial intermediaries rapidly increased their reliance on securitization using all sorts of financial assets. According to the Federal Reserve's flow of funds data, the liabilities of asset-backed security issuers "grew at a compound annual rate of forty-six percent from 1982 to 1999, and the non-mortgage segment of those issues grew at a compound annual rate of fifty-five percent."[178] Few people realize, though, that commercial banks, not nonbank "Wall Street" firms, are at the heart of this securitization process. In 2012, a Federal Reserve report affirmed that "banks are by far the predominant force in the securitization market," and that banks were "a significant force in these shadow banking segments related to securitization all along."[179] From 1990 to 2008, commercial banks' market share for the principal functions of securitization—including issuing, trustee services, underwriting, and servicing—remained well above 90 percent.[180]

MUTUAL FUNDS

A mutual fund is an SEC-registered investment company that pools money from many investors. The investors own mutual fund shares, which represent a proportionate ownership of the mutual fund's portfolio and the income the investments generate. Mutual funds are managed by SEC-registered investment advisers.

Investors in mutual funds buy their shares from and sell their shares to the mutual funds themselves, either directly or indirectly through a broker. A sale is known as a "redemption." The share price is determined on the basis of the value of the mutual fund's assets minus its liabilities, also known as the net asset value.[181] This pricing happens once per business day, typically after US stock exchanges close.

Most mutual funds hold equities, but mutual funds can hold both bonds and equities or can function as a money market mutual fund (described in the next subsection).[182] Mutual funds pursue diverse strategies, focusing on a particular industry or region or other theme, such as following an index. Most mutual funds follow long-only strategies (i.e., investing in securities with the expectation that their value will rise), but some funds pursue more complex strategies, such as long/short or using derivatives. As a general matter, the more complicated the strategy that a fund pursues—and the more the fund's success depends on the skill of its managers—the higher the fee it will charge investors.

Mutual funds are an extremely popular investment, especially for long-term investments, such as retirement savings, by American households.[183] Mutual funds are largely used by retail—or individual—investors, who hold 88 percent of the $22.1 trillion in US mutual fund net assets.[184] In 2022, more than 115 million individual investors and 68 million US households owned mutual funds.[185]

Some of this popularity stems from the fact that mutual funds have been viewed as a cost-effective method for individual investors to obtain some degree of diversification. Because mutual funds hold a basket of investments, retail investors can more easily hold many different investments through the fund without having to manage a wide variety of individual securities holdings themselves.

While traditional equity mutual funds remain popular, index mutual funds—which hold all, or a representative sample, of the securities in a specified index—are gaining in popularity.[186] Approximately half of households that own mutual funds owned at least one index mutual fund in 2022, and index mutual funds managed total net assets of $4.8 trillion across 517 funds.[187]

MONEY MARKET MUTUAL FUNDS

Money market mutual funds (MMFs), which were first introduced in 1971, represent just one of the many types of mutual funds, intermediaries that pool investors' funds to buy a portfolio of investments.[188] MMFs issue shares, and investors buy shares of the total portfolio.

MMFs pool investors' money to purchase only short-term (money market) instruments, such as Treasury securities, large-denomination certificates of deposit from banks, commercial paper, and repos.[189] Most of these securities are either federally backed, collateralized by federally backed securities, or guaranteed by banks that are federally insured. Whereas some MMFs cater to institutional investors, others offer investment opportunities to smaller retail customers.

Government MMFs invest mainly in government securities, tax-exempt MMFs invest mostly in state or local government debt securities, and prime MMFs invest in a broader range of money market instruments. Although MMFs held almost half of the outstanding commercial paper in the early 2000s, their investments in commercial paper have fallen in recent years. For instance, they held just 22 percent of the total amount outstanding in June 2020.[190]

In 2020, MMFs accounted for 22 percent of all repo *lending*, but MMFs generally do not borrow in the repo market.[191] That is, MMFs invest their shareholders' cash by lending in the repo market, just as other firms invest their cash. According to the SEC, approximately 70 percent of MMF repos are either for overnight maturities or can be terminated at any time, and another 24 percent have maturities between one and seven days.[192] Because MMFs invest in highly liquid short-term securities, they typically offer investors limited check-writing privileges like those offered by commercial banks on deposit accounts.[193] In fact, an increasing number of commercial banks have sponsored MMFs since the 1980s.

Bank-sponsored *prime* institutional MMFs, for instance, grew from an almost imperceptible share of the industry in 1986 to almost half ($227 billion) of all prime institutional MMF assets by the year 2000, and they further increased to 52 percent ($612 billion) by the end of 2007.[194] As with commercial paper, banks provide explicit guarantees for their conduits that create MMFs, thus increasing the liabilities for the commercial banking sector.

EXCHANGE-TRADED FUNDS

An exchange-traded fund, or ETF, is a basket of securities that investors can buy or sell on an exchange. ETFs are registered with the SEC as either open-end funds or unit investment trusts.[195] Importantly, an ETF is not a mutual fund, although many retail investors use ETFs and mutual funds in their portfolios for similar reasons. ETFs combine features of mutual funds—including the pooling of investor money to purchase a professionally managed basket of securities—with the ability to trade throughout the day on a national securities exchange at market prices.

Although ETFs, which were first offered in the 1990s, were initially designed to track equity indexes, a much wider variety of ETFs are offered today, including those that track fixed-income instruments or foreign securities. Other ETFs do not track indexes at all and instead are actively managed. ETFs may also offer leverage or try to move in the opposite direction of some benchmark, known as an inverse ETF. Because ETFs trade at their market price, the price they are trading at may not match the net asset value of the securities in the fund. The market value and the net asset value of an ETF are generally kept in line through arbitrage trading, whereby traders take advantage of the difference between the two prices to buy or sell the ETF or the securities it holds.

ETFs have grown in popularity, often at the expense of mutual funds, because they generally charge lower fees than mutual funds (due to differences in how they are distributed and lower transaction costs) and may also pay dividends to investors from the stocks the fund holds.[196] Like mutual funds, retail investors use ETFs to save for retirement or other financial goals, and institutional investors also use ETFs at an increasing rate because ETFs are generally low-fee, liquid investment vehicles. Retail investor trading activity accounted for approximately 15 percent of ETF trading volume, with approximately 12 percent of US households holding ETFs in 2022.[197]

In 2022, US ETFs totaled about $6.5 trillion in net assets.[198] More than 2,800 ETFs traded in 2022, a number that has been steadily increasing.[199]

Despite the growth in ETFs, mutual funds remain a much larger segment of the investment fund market. It is not uncommon for investors to have both mutual funds and ETFs in their portfolios. In fact, 82 percent of households that own ETFs also own mutual funds.[200]

PRIVATE FUNDS (HEDGE FUNDS AND PRIVATE EQUITY FUNDS)

A private fund is a pooled investment vehicle that issues securities and is primarily engaged in the business of investing in securities. Private funds are subject to less regulation—and generally provide less disclosure—than registered investment companies. Private funds are structured to qualify for exemptions from registration under the Investment Company Act, including exemptions for funds that have no more than 100 beneficial owners and funds that are limited to investors meeting the definition of a "qualified purchaser."[201] In practice, investment in most private funds is available only to large financial institutions (including pension funds) and high (or very high)-net-worth individuals.

In 2022, there were over 55,000 private funds in the United States, and the number of private funds and assets in private funds has been consistently growing over the past decade.[202] Most private funds are small; over one-third of funds had less than $25 million in assets in 2022, and more than half had less than $100 million.[203]

There are many different types of private funds, such as private equity funds, hedge funds, real estate funds, securitized asset funds, and venture capital funds. Funds within each of these categories may pursue a wide variety of investment strategies. Most private investment funds have limited liquidity, requiring investors to keep their money in the fund for a certain time and allowing withdrawals to occur only at certain preset intervals, such as quarterly or biannually. Private investment funds generally charge higher fees than registered investment companies; a common, though not universal, form of that fee is to charge the investor what is known as "2 and 20"—a management fee of 2 percent of the assets under management and a performance fee of 20 percent of the profits made by the fund above a certain predetermined point.

Hedge funds and private equity funds are the most common types of private funds, and hedge funds hold more assets than private equity funds.

In 2022, hedge funds accounted for almost 44 percent of private fund assets.[204] Hedge funds held an average of $746 million in assets, whereas private equity funds held an average of $283 million.[205] But while private equity funds tend to be smaller, there are a lot more of them. In 2022, private equity funds accounted for 44 percent of all private funds.[206]

Although often lumped together when discussing private investment funds, hedge funds and private equity funds are very different.

A hedge fund is an actively managed investment pool that can undertake a wide range of investment strategies to make a positive investment return for its investors. The term "hedge" comes from the fact that the fund's managers often seek to hedge bets within the fund, often investing in strategies that may offset one another. A common strategy for a fund is to use short selling, leverage, or derivatives to attempt to insulate the portfolio's return from some level of market risk. Regulation generally prohibits these types of strategies from being used by mutual funds or other investment funds that are generally available to public investors, which is one reason that hedge funds are considered to be higher-risk investments than such funds.

There are many different types of hedge funds. Hedge funds often seek to provide investors with returns that are not correlated with standard market indexes and, as such, are used by investors to add some level of diversification to their portfolio. Some hedge funds focus on particular types of investments, like equities, fixed-income securities, commodities, derivatives, or real estate. Some focus on particular industries or sectors. Some focus on a particular investment style, like a long/short hedge fund where the fund may take long positions on one company and short positions on a competitor based on the companies' relative valuations. Others may operate as an event-driven hedge fund that takes advantage of temporary stock mispricing created by corporate events like mergers or bankruptcies. Some focus on an activist strategy in which the fund aims to invest in a business with the intention of convincing the business to make changes, such as cutting costs, that increase the investment's value. Investors are often drawn to a particular hedge fund because of the perceived investing prowess of the fund's manager, who takes an active role in creating and maintaining the fund's portfolio.

As of 2022, hedge funds had $9.28 trillion in assets under management.[207] And although the total assets under management for hedge funds have been growing over the past decade, the share of private fund assets invested in hedge funds declined over the past 10 years from 57.2 percent in 2012 to 43.9 percent of private fund assets in 2022.[208]

Private equity funds, on the other hand, have increased as a percentage of total private fund assets from 21 percent in 2012 to almost 33 percent in 2022.[209] Private equity funds had $6.94 trillion in assets in 2022, and the number of private equity funds has increased by more than 2.8 times in the past 10 years.[210]

A private equity fund, like other private funds, is a pooled investment vehicle managed by an adviser who uses the funds to make investments. Unlike other private funds, however, a private equity fund focuses on long-term investment opportunities (often 10 years), and investors have extremely limited, if any, opportunities to withdraw their funds before the completion of the investment project.

Private equity funds typically take a controlling interest in an operating company and actively engage in the management of the company in order to increase its value. This approach is very different from a hedge fund, which is generally not involved in the management of the companies in which it is invested.[211] In this way, private equity funds often take on the role of business adviser, providing mentorship and industry expertise to the companies in which they invest.

In addition to specializing in certain industries or sectors, private equity funds can specialize in certain types of investment strategies. One such specialization is in buyouts, whereby a private equity firm buys a mature company with the hope of selling it later at a profit. It is the most common type of private equity strategy and is often thought of as synonymous with the private equity concept. Buyouts can be of private companies or public companies taken private through the purchase. They can be financed solely by capital from the fund or in conjunction with borrowed money; the latter case is known as a "leveraged buyout."

However, private equity funds can have other specializations. Another private equity specialization is in venture capital, where private equity supplies capital to an early-stage startup company. A private equity fund following a venture capital strategy often does not take a majority ownership stake in the company but still provides substantial mentorship and expertise to the growing firm. These funds are often referred to as venture capital funds—a specific term of art in the Investment Company Act to describe funds that have less than $10 million in assets and no more than 250 beneficial owners.[212]

In both circumstances, whether buying a mature company or supporting a growing one, the private equity fund provides capital to a company in need. And by providing strategic expertise to those companies, with the intention of making the investment profitable, private equity firms provide more than just financial capital.

Like other private investment funds, private equity investments tend to be higher risk than investments in public equities. However, they provide other advantages to investors, including portfolio diversification, the potential for greater returns, and a better alignment of interest between investors and the management of the company they invest in.[213]

DERIVATIVES

A derivative is a financial contract based on the value of an underlying asset, group of assets, or benchmark. The underlying asset for a derivative can be stocks, bonds, commodities, currencies, interest rates, or indexes. These financial instruments are generally used to help protect against risks, by allowing parties to trade specific financial risks with other parties who are more willing, or better suited, to take on the risk. Others use derivatives to engage in speculation about changes in the value of the underlying asset and thus provide liquidity to the market for others, especially those using the instruments to hedge against changes in value of the underlying asset.[214] But whether used for hedging or speculation, the general function of derivatives is to move risk, and its accompanying rewards, from the risk-averse to those with a higher risk tolerance.

There are many different types of derivatives, but they generally fall into four main categories: options, futures, forwards, and swaps. Derivatives are used primarily by institutional investors, not individuals, although the options market is an exception to that rule.

An options contract gives the buyer the opportunity to buy or sell the underlying asset at a price set out in the contract by a particular date (depending on the type of contract held). Options can be thought of as being similar to insurance contracts, whereby an upfront premium is paid against an undesirable outcome. Options are useful as a means of hedging an investor's position. For example, an options contract can be used to limit losses when an investor holds shares but purchases an options contract to provide a floor price for selling the shares.

Options trading also provides investors tools to engage in arbitrage (the attempt to profit from a difference in prices in, for example, separate markets) and the ability to earn income on shares that they own. In addition, because options usually cost a fraction of the price of the underlying shares, they also offer a more economical way to speculate on a security's price than by purchasing shares themselves. Options contracts can be written on a variety of underlying assets, including equities, indexes, interest rates, commodities, and currencies.

Options contracts are standardized and can be traded on exchanges. In fact, in 2022, 11.44 billion options contracts were traded on US exchanges.[215] Retail investors participate in these markets at nearly equal rates to institutional investors, with the retail share of equity options trading ranging from about 40 to 45 percent between 2020 and 2023.[216]

Futures are also standardized contracts that are traded on exchanges, but retail investors play only a small part in that market.[217] A futures contract is an agreement to buy or sell a particular asset at a predetermined price at a specified time in the future. A future is different from an option because an option gives an investor *the right* to buy or sell, whereas a future creates *an obligation* for the investor to buy or sell.

Futures contracts are used to set prices on a wide variety of commodities and financial instruments. Standardized commodity futures contracts began with the trading of grain futures on the Chicago Board of Trade in 1865. Today, there are several main types of commodity futures, including agricultural products, metals, energy, and transport. Commodity futures contracts are often used by producers or users of an underlying asset to hedge or guarantee the price at which the commodity is sold or purchased. Farmers, airlines, manufacturing companies, and oil producers, among many others, use the futures markets to lock in prices for commodities that they produce or consume. Commodity futures can also be used by speculators who want to use the contract to bet on the price of the underlying asset.

Futures contracts on financial assets are more recent—first traded on the Chicago Mercantile Exchange in 1972—but today they make up an even larger portion of the futures market than commodity futures.[218] Financial futures are based on the future value of a security or index, and they are popular instruments to hedge the risks of interest-rate changes, exchange-rate movements, and share-price changes.[219] Futures contract volume in 2023 for North America, for which the United States is the largest component, was about 5.3 billion contracts.[220]

Other derivatives are not traded on exchanges and instead are traded "over the counter." These derivatives are not standardized, and the transactions are privately negotiated between two parties without the inter-mediation of an exchange. These financial instruments are almost exclusively used by institutions and financially sophisticated parties. Forwards are one type of over-the-counter (OTC) derivative. Forwards are similar to futures in that they are agreements on the specific price and quantity of an underlying asset to be paid in the future. But forwards are individually negotiated, and there are differences in the risks between the two parties because there is no exchange involved to intermediate the contract.

A swap is another type of OTC derivative, although the 2010 Dodd-Frank Act required many swaps to trade through a swap execution facility.[221] Swaps are derivative contracts whereby two parties agree to exchange cash flows or liabilities from two different financial instruments. Unlike a forward, which requires one payment between the parties, swaps generally obligate the parties to make a series of payments. The most commonly used swaps hedge against interest-rate risk, but swaps can be used to hedge against credit risk, foreign exchange risk, default on credit by a third party, and the prices of commodities, among other things.

Different types of derivatives offer different choices to investors. The structure of the contract—that is, the type of instrument used—can make a big difference in terms of transaction costs, credit risk, leverage, or other terms to the parties of the agreement. Famed investor Warren Buffett once described derivatives as "financial weapons of mass destruction."[222] It is certainly true that derivatives can be risky, complex, and difficult to understand; however, they serve a real function in managing risk.

CONCLUSION

This chapter provided an overview of the depth and breadth of US financial markets. Without such robust financial markets, obtaining the goods and services that improve living standards would be much more difficult and expensive precisely because financial markets help people direct scarce resources to their most productive uses. Nonetheless, financial markets have a long history of being blamed for all kinds of social and economic problems. Whereas the preceding chapters have discussed some of these instances, the next chapter goes into much more detail. It demonstrates that critiques of financial markets are as old as financial markets themselves, and that most of the modern critiques of finance rest on weak foundations.

Chapter 4

Financial Market Critics (Still) Miss the Mark

US financial markets are a central reason that the US economy is as productive as it is. As people buy and sell multiple financial instruments, money flows through financial institutions, and people direct limited resources to their most productive uses. Without robust financial markets, this process would be more difficult, and obtaining the goods and services that improve living standards would be more difficult and expensive. Put simply, a poorly functioning financial sector results in a society with fewer goods and services, fewer employment opportunities, and lower incomes. Still, an incredibly long tradition of criticizing financial markets exists around the world, and no shortage of Americans have taken part in it.

For instance, in 2023, political commentator Tucker Carlson fiercely critiqued America's economy and financial markets. On Glenn Greenwald's *System Update* Rumble show, Carlson claimed, "Libertarian economics was a scam perpetrated by the beneficiaries of the economic system that they were defending, so they created this whole intellectual framework to justify the private equity culture that's hollowed out the country." Carlson then complained that this culture has produced a bad economic system for Americans as evidenced by the proliferation of deep-discount stores like Dollar General. As he sees it, the spread of such dollar stores "degrades people and it makes their lives worse, and it increases exponentially the amount of ugliness in your society."[223]

Carlson's critique of the financial industry is not an isolated case among pundits, politicians, or even the academy. In recent years, various members of these groups have criticized everything from small-dollar loans to corporate share repurchases. Their targets include private equity firms, hedge funds, leveraged buyouts, short selling, securitized assets, and, of course, the omnipresent *Wall Street*. Although these complaints are firmly rooted in the Great Depression era, when complaints of excessive speculation and market manipulation blossomed, the roots go much deeper.

BABYLONIANS AND MEDIEVAL CATHOLICS SET THE STAGE

Americans' concerns over excessive speculation, and their suspicion of speculators, have been prevalent for the past few centuries. These fears did not, however, spontaneously emerge during the 18th century. Rather, they arose from views that developed throughout the world over thousands of years, along with finance and commerce. Some of the oldest surviving documents known trace these roots to the second millennium BCE, sometimes referred to as the Old Babylonian period. By that time, people had created a basic financial system that included mortgages, land deeds, and even promissory notes.[224] Believe it or not, attacks on "financiers" date at least as far back to this period.[225] Then, as now, finance had the *potential* for lifting people out of poverty and affecting major social changes, so it was a threat to the ruling class. Just as importantly, people recognized the hardships that debtors could face.

Today, it is common to refer to someone being "trapped" in debt. In ancient Babylon, however, the term could have been used quite literally. During this period, people had the right to sell themselves into slavery as a collateral for a loan, and debtors were sometimes forced to sell themselves into slavery to ensure repayment.[226] Obviously, it would be difficult to argue that such a system made life for the common citizen anything but miserable. It can hardly be surprising, then, that lending was controversial.

Political leaders commonly used loan forgiveness edicts during this period as political tools, and one surviving tablet includes such a proclamation that demonizes financiers, grouping usurers with criminals that should be thrown out of the city.[227] Still, the earliest known laws from this period show that political leaders chose to regulate charging interest for loans, which had long been derided as "usury," rather than to prohibit it.[228] For instance, the Code of Hammurabi, named for a famous Babylonian ruler who lived circa 1800 BCE, created a comprehensive framework for commerce. It included limits of terms on debt contracts of three years, as well as maximum rates of interest on silver and barley of 20 percent and 33⅓ percent, respectively.[229]

The widespread concern with usury had both social and economic implications. Closer to the end of the BCE period, philosophers Plato and Aristotle both spoke out against usury. According to Aristotle: "The most hated sort [of money making], and with the greatest reason, is usury, which makes a gain out of money itself, and not from the natural use of it. For money was intended to be used in exchange, but not to increase at interest."[230] Aristotle argued that because money does not reproduce on its own, if someone gains during a monetary exchange, then it must be "at the expense of other men."[231] In other words, Aristotle believed that when a monetary exchange results in profit from something other than the production of goods, one party wins and the other loses.

By the medieval period, there was a clearer connection between usury laws and broader economic issues. The medieval Scholastics, a group of Christian scholars, accepted Aristotle's interpretation of finance as an unnatural phenomenon.[232] Their teachings reflected a similar apprehension with profiting from lending, which they equated with the sale of a nonproductive asset.[233] They believed that this kind of activity led to a redistribution of assets and violated the ethical principle of reciprocity. Thus, uncontrolled, it would increase the concentration of both economic and political power, a situation the Scholastics viewed as unsustainable.[234] Importantly, the medieval Catholic Church accepted the Scholastics' views on usury, leading it to institute a prohibition on charging interest.[235]

Many scholars have interpreted this prohibition as at least partly a religious institutional backlash against finance and commerce in the early medieval period. In medieval Venice and rival cities, for instance, flourishing commercial and financial activity threatened to upend the Church-centric social order.[236] Regardless, the Church explicitly taught that lenders *could* charge interest for the reimbursement of *legitimate* expenses.[237] Legitimate expenses were those tied to so-called productive assets, whereas making a "gain out of money itself" was not viewed as a productive use. Until roughly 1300 CE, the main arguments given for prohibiting usury were (a) money is not a productive asset, (b) money is a fixed medium of exchange and can only be sold for its fixed price, and (c) the ownership of money means nothing more than the right to use the money to buy things so one cannot charge separately for the use and ownership of money.[238]

This reasoning is problematic, because there is no objective way to define legitimate or productive use. By their very nature, these terms are subjective. Anyone could easily view, for instance, pet rocks, sweaters for dogs, breakfast cereal, or fruit pouches as consumer products that *waste* productive assets.[239] By implication, any business venture to produce these products would be deemed nonproductive. Moreover, borrowed funds, as well as profits from lending, could ultimately be used for purposes categorized as legitimate even if their *initial* use was deemed illegitimate. Moreover, the value of money is no more fixed than the value of the goods and services it is used to buy.

Nonetheless, the Church and the Scholastics tried to make a sharp distinction between financing and investing. They argued that money's role in investing in physical capital, not the acquisition of money, is what makes money productive.[240] In the 13th century, Pope Innocent IV directly connected usury to underinvestment.[241] He argued:

> If usury were permitted, all rich persons would rather put their money safely in a usurious loan than invest in agriculture. Only the poor would be left to do the farming and then they would not possess the animals and tools with which to farm. Famine would result.[242]

For whatever reason, by 1750 the Scholastics had changed their views, and the Church officially changed its position through a series of decisions between 1822 and 1836. According to renowned Catholic scholar

John T. Noonan Jr., these decisions removed "all doubts and practical difficulties by publicly decreeing that the interest allowed by law may be taken by everyone."[243] Thus, as times changed, the lending of money itself came to be seen as productive. Still, this change was controversial, and negative views toward usury and finance did not disappear, even after the world's first stock exchange formed.

Box 4.1: Leveraged buyouts were not invented in the 1980s

As the US economy has grown, leveraged buyouts (LBOs) as a method of financing, and the number of people employing them (including private equity firms), have grown as well. But it is wrong to think that the LBO is a recent invention.[a]

In 1901, the banker J. P. Morgan merged nine steel companies to create the United States Steel Corporation. The deal created the world's largest corporation at that time, valued at $1.4 billion. Morgan financed the deal with more than one-third debt, an amount well above the norm at that time.[b] In 1919, Henry Ford needed $75 million to regain control of Ford Motor Company, which he had founded. Though he had never previously borrowed money, he funded the buyout with $70 million in short-term bonds and $5 million in bank financing.[c] Demand for cars slumped soon after his buyout, and Ford had to cut costs to pay his debts—which he did by, among other methods, letting go of employees, selling equipment, and pushing unsold inventory onto dealers.[d] Eventually, though, the company survived and thrived.

Although many explanations have been given for the initial wave of LBOs in the 1980s, no *single* factor appears to be driving that increase. However, a study that examined almost 1,200 LBO deals between 1980 and 2008 shows that the cost of borrowing has been a main driver of the increased use of various types of debt in leveraged buyouts.[e] Moreover, although it is difficult to obtain a consistent time

(continued)

Box 4.1 *(continued)*

series, research on LBO exit characteristics—the term "exit" refers to the end of the private equity firm's contractual obligation with the company it bought—suggests that between 1970 and 2007, bankruptcies occurred in just 6 percent of deals, without any obvious increasing trend.[f] In other words, during this period, private equity firms saved almost 95 percent of the companies that they purchased using LBOs.

Separately, research published in *the Review of Corporate Finance Studies* in 2021, using data from 1997 to 2009, reports that there were very small differences in debt default frequencies among non-private-equity-backed firms, private-equity-backed firms, and private equity-exited firms. Moreover, while private equity-backed firms did have a slightly higher probability of a default, controlling for the companies' credit rating erases the difference, with private equity-exited firms having a *lower* probability of a default.[g] These findings are consistent with private equity firms buying riskier companies and, in many cases, saving them from disbanding through either bankruptcy or liquidation.

MARX AND KEYNES CARRY ON THE TRADITION

The Amsterdam Exchange, founded in the early 17th century, is generally considered to be the world's first stock market.[244] By the late 17th century, traders were engaged in short selling, and using put and call options. The exchange was known for enabling even small investors to speculate in fractions of shares.[245] As the 18th century unfolded, the Dutch "led the way in developing increasingly sophisticated financial instruments," and the American Revolution became a major force in the development of a new transatlantic financial system.[246] The economic and social changes during this period were amazing, but they hardly compared with what was to come in the latter half of the 19th century and in the 20th century. Against this backdrop of change, criticism of financial markets grew right along with the economy.

In 1867, Karl Marx published *Das Kapital* (*Capital*), a voluminous work born out of reaction to the industrializing world he experienced. While *Capital* has been widely discussed and debated, Marx's views on modern finance are sometimes overlooked. Yet some of his views on finance sound like those of an angry Scholastic philosopher. For instance, in Volume 1, he criticizes the medieval Venetian system of public debt by labeling bond traders a "class of lazy annuitants" who just shuffled money around.[247] He argued, "As with the stroke of an enchanter's wand," this system "endows barren money with the power of breeding and thus turns it into capital, without the necessity of its exposing itself to the troubles and risks inseparable from its employment in industry or even in usury."[248] He also complains that the system created "the improvised wealth of the financiers," and that it gave "rise to joint-stock companies, to dealings in negotiable effects of all kinds, and to agiotage [speculative dealing in foreign currencies], in a word to stock-exchange gambling and the modern bankocracy."[249]

During the Great Depression, there was no shortage of people who believed that Marx had correctly predicted the downfall of capitalism.[250] Perhaps less appreciated, though, is that his analogy between *financial markets* and gambling closely resembles one made by John Maynard Keynes during the Great Depression. In his 1936 treatise on economics, Keynes chastised speculators and scornfully likened their activities to casino gambling:

> Speculators may do no harm as bubbles on a steady stream of enterprise. But the position is serious when enterprise becomes the bubble on a whirlpool of speculation. When the capital development of a country becomes a by-product of the activities of a casino, the job is likely to be ill-done.[251]

According to Keynes, financial markets had functioned more efficiently in previous decades because, before the 1920s, share ownership was more concentrated among corporate managers and people with "special knowledge" rather than the general public.[252] Yet Keynes provided no evidence for his hypothesis—that more widely dispersed share ownership had caused the stock market to become "overvalued" in 1929.

Moreover, the trend toward more dispersed ownership was hardly new, dating to at least the 17th century.[253]

Keynes himself regularly speculated, but he discouraged widespread access to the markets.[254] He argued:

> It is usually agreed that casinos should, in the public interest, be inaccessible and expensive. And perhaps the same is true of Stock Exchanges. That the sins of the London Stock Exchange are less than those of Wall Street . . . not so much to differences in national character, as to the fact that to the average Englishman Throgmorton Street is, compared with Wall Street to the average American, inaccessible and very expensive.[255]

Keynes even proposed a tax to make the average American less likely to engage in stock market investing. He called for a "substantial government transfer tax on all transactions" to diminish "the predominance of speculation over enterprise in the United States."[256]

One problem with Keynes's reasoning has been ignored by market critics for centuries: there is no objective difference between financing "speculation" and "enterprise."[257] Keynes likely recognized this problem, though, and his preferred policy prescription was to impose a blanket tax on all financial transactions rather than to authorize government officials to determine which investments were speculative. Presumably, the tax would sufficiently reduce "speculation" because it would make it more difficult for less wealthy members of the public to enter the markets. Regardless, suggesting such a proposal while offering no evidence that broader ownership in American stocks caused the 1929 crash, or the Depression, is a puzzling choice for any economist.

Nonetheless, Keynes was not the only famous 20th-century economist to make such a mistake. In the 1980s, Nobel Prize–winning economist James Tobin echoed several of Keynes's anti-speculation themes and even proposed a similar transaction tax. Yet like Keynes's in the 1930s, Tobin's critiques of financial markets amounted to little more than his own negative opinions. For example, in 1984, he lamented the "speculations on the speculations of other speculators" and corporate managers' excessive concern with "short run performances" rather than long-run value creation.[258] Still, Tobin never explained how one might know, just for instance, the true long-run value of various assets, including those he thought were priced "with negligible fundamentals."[259]

Tobin also took aim at derivatives because they did little more than increase leverage.[260] Tobin, however, ignored the fact that derivatives also allow people to reduce their financial risk to all kinds of unexpected commercial activities while devoting minimal resources. They can protect themselves against agriculture price declines, for example, without having to purchase raw commodities. Moreover, attempts to distinguish between this group and Tobin's "speculators and arbitrageurs" remain subjective—and as problematic for policymaking—as they were in the 18th century. Still, Tobin doubled down with his own version of the age-old critique that financial markets are wasteful unless they finance investment in "real" assets. He argued:

> What is clear is that very little of the work done by the securities industry, as gauged by the volume of market activity, has to do with the financing of real investment in any very direct way. Likewise, those markets have very little to do, in aggregate, with the translation of the saving of households into corporate business investment.[261]

Much like Keynes, Tobin did little more than provide his opinion on the supposedly wasteful nature of financial markets. The fact that secondary-market activity does not directly finance capital investment was well-known centuries before Tobin's critique, as was the fact that such activity *indirectly* helps people direct capital to its most productive use. Moreover, Tobin failed to provide any evidence that the "volume of market activity" in the securities industry harmed "corporate business investment."

In much the same fashion, many of these themes showed up in a widely cited 1985 *Business Week* article titled "The Casino Society: Playing with Fire," in which author and reporter Anthony Bianco bemoans virtually every aspect of US financial markets. Bianco complains, for instance, about the supposedly excessive volume of shares traded each day on the New York Stock Exchange, which was 108 million in 1985. He criticizes debt-based corporate takeovers known as leveraged buyouts, particularly those financed with high-risk ("junk") bonds, as well as the ability to "play the stock market without owning a share."[262]

Bianco claims that the United States "has evolved into what Lord Keynes might have called a 'casino society'—a nation obsessively devoted to high-stakes financial maneuvering as a shortcut to wealth." Although Bianco acknowledges that the US economy and financial markets "grew up together," he offers little praise for finance. Instead, he claims that "their symbiotic relationship has been thrown out of whack by the advent of the casino society," and that "the volume of financial transactions . . . has soared beyond calculation—and beyond economic purpose." Like Keynes and Tobin, Bianco fails to support most of his claims, including that market volume had soared beyond economic purpose.

Aside from ignoring the broad economic growth that had taken place up to their time, the core problem with Keynes's, Tobin's, and Bianco's critiques is their failure to specify what the optimal levels of financial activity or investment in real goods should be. Both Keynes and Tobin attempt to avoid the question of optimality by calling for a blanket transaction tax to stem all financial market activity, but that's not a solution. Implementing their policy would blindly cause a reduction in investment in the real economy, and the question of how much is all that remains. It makes little sense to implement such a policy and risk lowering productivity, increasing the cost of living, and reducing people's opportunities to earn a living and build wealth, merely based on someone's view that there is "too much speculation" in financial markets. It is incumbent upon anyone calling for such a tax to demonstrate its potential costs and specify optimal outcomes rather than simply opine that there is "too much speculation."[263]

On the surface, historical context makes these three critics' arguments look even worse. For instance, Keynes, Tobin, and Bianco all ignore US population growth. This omission alone is a major weakness because the population went from 50 million in 1880 to 122 million in 1929, and then to 238 million by 1985. The size of the US market—that is, its number of consumers—essentially doubled between the end of Reconstruction and the onset of the Great Depression, and again between World War II and 1985. This growth alone makes it at least plausible that financial transactions grew as would be expected in the

Box 4.2: There is no reason to ban share repurchases

Many critics of share repurchases (stock buybacks) want to restrict or ban them based on the idea that companies repurchase their own shares *instead* of investing in projects that would otherwise provide jobs and increase economic activity. A major problem with this underinvestment critique is that the empirical evidence shows buybacks have *not* systematically reduced corporate investment.[a] Indeed, aggregate investment—even if broken down into smaller investment *categories*, including research and development—has been steadily rising as a portion of gross domestic product.[b] Additionally, the Securities and Exchange Commission (SEC) has acknowledged that, in real terms, gross share repurchases did *not* appreciably spike after the 1982 rule that clarified the terms of their use; they remained relatively flat between 1983 and 1995, never surpassing $100 billion.[c] However, gross repurchases did eventually start an increasing trend, but only after a spike in overall market capitalization in the late 1990s.

Although *net* share repurchases also started an upward trend around the same time, the value of buybacks relative to market capitalization, in both net and gross terms, remained relatively constant from 1983 to 2019.[d] Additionally, although net repurchases were negative in several years before 2001, the ratio of net repurchases to market capitalization otherwise remained flat—between zero and approximately 2 percent—from 1983 to 2019.[e]

Some advocates of banning or restricting stock buybacks have mistakenly claimed that share repurchases were illegal before the 1980s, and that their use exploded only after the SEC finalized a new rule in 1982. For instance, in 2023, American Compass called for a ban on stock buybacks and claimed that stock buybacks were "illegal until the SEC promulgated Rule 10b-18 in 1982 to provide them safe harbor from insider trading prohibitions."[f]

This claim is incorrect; stock buybacks were not previously illegal and the SEC's Rule 10b-18 did not provide corporations with a

(continued)

Box 4.2 *(continued)*

safe harbor from insider trading prohibitions. Before the 1982 rule,
as markets grew in both volume and value, corporations increasingly
relied on them to return capital to shareholders. As a result, they
were increasingly accused of manipulating their share prices, and
were worried that they would run afoul of the anti-manipulation
provisions of the Securities Exchange Act of 1934.[g] The 1982 rule
provided a safe harbor from liability for stock price manipulation,
but not if the share repurchases are "fraudulent or manipulative."
It is also worth noting that insider trading is distinct from market
manipulation and fraud.[h] Importantly, in 2020, the SEC acknowledged that both market data and the academic literature suggest that
most buybacks are not motivated by a desire to manipulate a company's stock price.[i]

Additionally, although there is no doubt that more companies began using share repurchases in the 1980s, it is well
documented that their usage first increased *in the 1960s.*[j] The
following passage from a 1966 *Journal of Finance* article provides
some perspective:

> A survey of the repurchasing activities of companies listed on the
> New York Stock Exchange revealed that in 1963, for example, 132
> firms "repurchased enough of their own common shares to account
> for 5 percent or more of the total trading in their securities." Share
> repurchasing was, in fact, such a popular corporate activity in 1963
> that "the total dollars spent by companies to buy back their com-
> mon shares was 30 percent greater than the amount which they
> raised through (new) equity issues."[k]

Aside from the empirical evidence, and the many legitimate
reasons a company might have to repurchase its shares, congressional
opponents of buybacks still mustered enough support—in the Inflation Reduction Act of 2022—to impose a new (1 percent) tax on the
value of corporate share repurchases.

United States, which, according to Bianco, has the world's "most boun-tiful economy" and the "most highly developed capital markets."[264]

Similarly, Tobin complains that "the *turnover* of stocks in the United States is greater than in any other country."[265] Yet Tobin ignores any of the valid economic reasons that might explain this higher turnover ratio, defined as the total value of shares traded relative to the average market capitalization. This omission is strange because the turnover ratio tends to be higher in more developed and larger countries.[266] (See figure 4.1.) Otherwise, this ratio doesn't provide any policy-relevant information—it is merely one measure of value-adjusted stock market volume.

Additionally, in hindsight, Bianco's critique of market volume looks, at best, wildly premature. Although he complained that a daily vol-ume of 108 million shares traded on the New York Stock Exchange was excessive, that number now stands near four *billion* shares.[267] Again, given the overall economic growth of the United States, this increase in volume is not surprising. Larger markets present more opportunities to issue both debt and equity, as well as more opportunities to earn income and build wealth, so it is not surprising to see more trading volume. Moreover, opportunity is not all that grew—Americans became much wealthier and earned higher incomes.

Figure 4.1: Turnover ratio by GDP, 2010

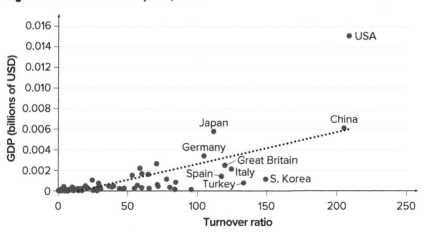

Source: World Bank, "Data Catalog" website.

Figure 4.2: GDP per capita in selected countries, in 2011 dollars

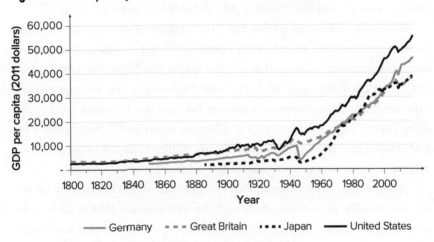

Source: Maddison Project, "Maddison Historical Statistics."

As figure 4.2 illustrates, Americans' per capita income surpassed that of the citizens of the other major developed nations in the early 20th century and remained higher into the 21st century. Even when one focuses on American GDP growth during the post–World War II era, the US economy has exhibited enormous growth. In real terms, the US economy was 4 times larger in 1985 than it was in 1947 and is currently 10 times its size in 1947.[268] Indeed, it would have been strange if American financial market activity had not rapidly increased during these growth periods.

Importantly, even as financial market activity displayed enormous growth throughout the post–World War II era, aggregate investment in the United States did not display a downward trend. Yet critics often rely on narrowly defined categories of investment and its subcomponents, as well as specially chosen time periods, to argue that American investment is in decline and below optimal levels.[269] Critics use similar tricks—picking and choosing certain metrics, time periods, and research findings, while ignoring others—to claim that the financial sector now represents a disproportionate share of the economy's profits, but the evidence does not support such claims.[270] (See figure 4.3.)

Figure 4.3: Share of corporate profits by financial, manufacturing, and nonfinancial less manufacturing

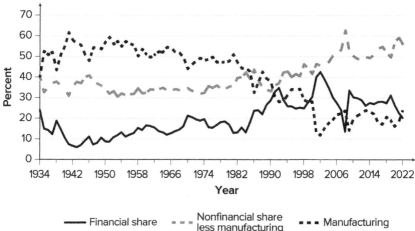

Source: Bureau of Economic Analysis, National Income and Product Accounts.

FINANCIAL MARKETS ARE INSEPARABLE FROM AMERICAN PROSPERITY

Financial market critics frequently ignore the symbiotic relationship between growth in financial markets and the overall economy. Instead, they focus on the negative aspects of taking economic and financial risks, often decrying the use of leveraged buyouts and share repurchases in the American economy. For instance, echoing Tucker Carlson's critique, a recent policy handbook by American Compass, a self-identified conservative public policy group, complains that the private equity industry's use of leveraged buyouts (LBOs) increases the risk of bankruptcy and that "it is the workers and communities reliant on those firms that bear the highest cost."[271] The truth, though, is that many of those firms would go bankrupt—or go bankrupt sooner—without the private equity LBOs, which does no favors for the "workers and communities reliant on those firms."

There is no doubt that, throughout history, excessive debt has caused some firms to file for bankruptcy. It is just as certain, though, that taking on high debt has *saved* many firms. Naturally, as the economy and financial markets have grown, the use of all kinds of debt has grown, including through leveraged buyouts.[272] Although Wall Street firms popularized LBOs in the 1980s, the basic mechanism—using massive amounts of debt to purchase a company—has been around for generations. Additionally, the evidence does not support the idea that private equity firms' use of LBOs increases the risk of bankruptcy.

Much like LBOs, corporate share repurchases, also known as stock buybacks, have long been a favorite target of financial market critics. In 2021, for instance, Sen. Elizabeth Warren (D-MA) claimed that when corporate managers decide to buy back their company's shares, they are simply "pumping up" their share price and deciding "not to invest in [the] business."[273] In 2019, Sen. Tammy Baldwin (D-WI) introduced legislation to "rein in" share buybacks and likened the practice to "the looting of the American corporation."[274] The same year, Sen. Marco Rubio (R-FL) blamed perceived corporate underinvestment on share buybacks and argued, "When [a] corporation uses profits for stock buy-back it's deciding that returning capital to shareholders is better for business than investing in their products or workers."[275]

It makes little sense to apply this negative view of the repurchase decision broadly to "the American corporation." First, it is mistaken to view corporate managers as being engaged in some kind of battle between shareholders, customers, and workers. If, for example, corporate managers consistently choose to send money to shareholders at the expense of investing in the equipment and workers needed to deliver the products that customers demand, the company would cease to exist.

Moreover, years of research have demonstrated that both share repurchases and dividends—two distinct methods of returning value to shareholders—temporarily decrease the firm's market value, with dividends lowering the share price and repurchases lowering the share count. Although the mix between dividends and repurchases changed between 1965 and 2021, shareholder returns have experienced no clear effect.[276] In other words, share repurchases do not prop up the value of the firm. In the absence of profitable investment opportunities, companies may choose to return cash to shareholders, thus ensuring that capital is employed more productively by allowing shareholders to choose where to reinvest that cash.[277] Overall, the evidence does not support the critics who want to restrict buybacks.

Box 4.3: Derivatives help both Main Street and Wall Street

Derivatives have been criticized for centuries, and they have unjustly earned a bad reputation. For instance, in his 1985 article, author Anthony Bianco derisively refers to derivatives as a "wasting asset" that becomes "worthless upon expiration," and because they allow people to play the stock market "without owning a share."[a] He singles out listed options as a "weapon in the markets" because they put "the trader in charge," and he frets that derivatives, including those tied to inflation, have "no direct connection to the factory floors of Main Street."

Yet it simply is not true that derivatives have no direct connection to production. Inflation affects the value of future sales for manufacturers, as well as their future input and capital costs, so it is beneficial to use derivatives to hedge against inflation. Similarly, multinational companies have long used derivatives to protect against unfavorable changes in exchange rates, and farmers regularly use derivatives to protect against changes in prices for their crops. The ability to hedge against such risks without regularly purchasing foreign currencies, or other commodities, enables firms to put scarce capital to more productive uses. Thus, in many cases, derivatives are just a form of insurance. In fact, the critique that derivatives give people exposure to certain assets without first buying those assets applies equally to insurance companies. Any fair evaluation of derivatives markets must consider these benefits.[b]

CONCLUSION

In 1998, Economics Nobel laureate Merton Miller argued that whether financial markets contribute to economic growth "is a proposition almost too obvious for serious discussion."[278] He also pointed out, though, that "because they draw so much publicity, particularly when they crash, [financial markets] have always been blamed for society's ills."[279] Given the historical record, it is difficult to argue with Miller on these points, especially the last one.

Centuries of history document a love–hate relationship with financial markets. The fact that finance literally enables people to take economic risks partly explains this relationship. Moreover, the people who most need financing are often those who find themselves in an unfavorable economic position. In many cases, they may lose their livelihood if they fail to secure financing even though borrowing more money is risky. Regardless, when people take risks, some inevitably end in failure, and people in such circumstances may remain liable for repaying debts even though they have lost their livelihood. Thus, it is not surprising that finance has always been controversial. This unfortunate aspect of finance partly explains how the regulatory framework for financial markets—the subject of the next chapter—has evolved.

The downside of taking economic risk has a built-in political appeal because human beings always look to political leaders to solve problems. Throughout American history, this dynamic has provided impetus for major changes to the financial regulatory framework, even outside crisis periods. Unfortunately, the results have often been dismal. Regulations have generally not made markets more stable or resilient, and they have often done the opposite. Along with this failure, financial regulations have consistently reduced Americans' ability to decide what to do with their own money. Even though the regulatory framework often provides a false sense of security, policymakers rarely consider rolling back even minor financial regulations, much less making wholesale changes to the framework.

Chapter 5

Overview of Modern
Financial Regulation

Economic and financial crises, like the Great Depression and the 2008 financial crisis, have typically spurred Congress to make major changes to America's financial regulatory framework. But Congress has also made many changes to the regulatory framework in ordinary times. In both crises and normal economic conditions, many of these changes were driven by popular support. In some cases, support ebbed and flowed over many decades, culminating in a policy change long after the original advocates were gone from the political scene—and the original major players were gone from the market. In others, current events propelled Congress to act. In almost all cases, though, these changes demonstrate the everlasting connection between politics and financial regulation, as well as the tendency to increase financial regulation.

OVERVIEW OF BANK REGULATION

Historically, regulators have managed banks' activities much more extensively than those of nonbanking financial firms. One major justification for extensively regulating banks' activities in this manner is to protect the Deposit Insurance Fund of the Federal Deposit Insurance Corporation (FDIC). More broadly, the justification has been to protect *taxpayers* because they are ultimately responsible for any FDIC-insured losses beyond the nominal balance in the Deposit Insurance Fund.

Bank regulations are also often justified by citing *systemic-risk* concerns. That is, policymakers fear that without strictly regulating banks' activities, the result would be widespread bank failures and, therefore, system-wide financial and economic instability.[280]

Although these justifications have influenced distinct regulatory frameworks for banks versus those for capital market firms, concepts such as "systemic risks," "financial stability," and "economic instability" can easily be used to justify more stringent regulations on all kinds of firms because they lack a common, objective, definition. In fact, the regulatory approaches in these two market segments have been moving in the same direction for decades, partly on the grounds of guarding against ill-defined systemic risks. As a result, two major long-term regulatory trends have arisen in the United States: (a) financial regulation has increased, and (b) regulators have taken on a more active role in managing financial firms' risks. These trends apply to both the banking and capital markets. This chapter addresses banking regulation first.

Banks' activities are highly regulated by both state and federal regulators, more so than most types of businesses. These regulatory functions can be broadly grouped as follows: (a) chartering and entry restrictions, (b) regulation and supervision, and (c) examination.[281] Chartering and entry restrictions include the regulatory process that people must follow to start a new bank, as well as the requirements that existing banks must comply with before they can expand into new geographic markets through mergers and acquisitions.

Supervision and examination authority are complementary, and they cover a much wider range of activities. Supervision involves both the initial publication of rules to implement statutory law, and less formal press releases and circulars known as "guidance." Additionally, regulators routinely examine banks' records to ensure that they are following the rules. At times, these examinations are informal regulatory sessions, but regulators sometimes use the process to implement changes to bank operations. For example, regulators can require banks to increase capital with threatened enforcement actions even during informal examinations. Banks tend to comply with regulators' informal suggestions because failure to do so can bring additional regulatory scrutiny or formal enforcement actions.[282]

In addition to the many laws, rules, and regulations, the US system is complicated because it has so many federal financial regulators, as well as state regulators. At the federal level, depending on the banking activity, at least eight regulators could supervise, examine, or otherwise regulate a bank: (a) Federal Reserve, (b) FDIC, (c) Office of the Comptroller of the Currency (OCC), (d) Consumer Financial Protection Bureau, (e) Federal Housing Finance Agency, (f) Commodity Futures Trading Commission (CFTC), (g) Securities and Exchange Commission (SEC), and (h) Financial Crimes Enforcement Network (FinCEN).[283]

In practice, both state- and federally chartered banks are subject to state laws governing the basic transactions in which they engage with their customers. For instance, state laws, most notably the Uniform Commercial Code, govern such practices as transactions in commercial paper and promissory notes, bank deposits, funds transfers, secured transactions, and contracts.[284] Other state laws govern bank chartering, safety and soundness, securities, insurance, real property, and mortgages.[285] However, federal law governs *federally* chartered banks' rights and obligations as corporate entities. Moreover, the bank regulatory framework is now more federalized than ever because any FDIC-insured state bank is prohibited from engaging in any activity impermissible for national banks—and nearly all state banks are FDIC insured.[286]

Under the current framework, most banks are supervised and examined by more than one regulator. In general, federally chartered banks are subject to supervision by the Office of the Comptroller of the Currency. State-chartered banks that are members of the Federal Reserve System are subject to oversight by both the Federal Reserve Board and by state regulators. Finally, non-Fed-member state-chartered banks that are insured by the FDIC are regulated by the FDIC and state regulators. Beginning in 1933, all banks—whether state or federally chartered—that join the Federal Reserve System are required to have FDIC deposit insurance, and the FDIC is, at the very least, a secondary regulator of all FDIC-insured banks.[287]

Another layer of complexity exists because the Fed is the primary regulator of all bank holding companies, the legal entity that can own multiple banks and financial firms.[288] Separately, a statutory formula dictates specific responsibilities for the various federal banking regulators. For example, the Federal Deposit Insurance Act defines the "appropriate Federal banking agency" for purposes of which agency regulates which bank, and determines which federal agency is responsible for approving bank mergers.[289]

Within this overall framework, federal regulators have an enormous amount of discretion in carrying out their responsibilities. Although some level of discretion is unavoidable in regulatory matters, broad discretion is problematic to the extent that it leads to uncertainty and gives regulators unchecked power over individuals and businesses. The following list provides a handful of ways that US banking law gives regulators discretion.[290]

- **The examination process and CAMELS ratings.** Depending on the size of the institution, federal regulators examine banks at least once every 18 months.[291] At these on-site examinations, regulators give each bank a CAMELS rating under the Uniform Financial Institutions Rating System.[292] The CAMELS acronym stands for capital adequacy, asset quality, management capability, earnings quality (and level), liquidity adequacy, and sensitivity to market risk.[293] Both individual component and composite ratings are given on a scale of 1 to 5, with 1 indicating the strongest rating and 5 the weakest.[294] Examiners have a great deal of discretion in calculating the CAMELS ratings, and they base each component rating on "a qualitative analysis of the factors comprising that component and its interrelationship with the other components."[295] A poor rating can affect a bank's ability to operate, as well as its operating costs. For instance, the composite CAMELS rating helps determine a bank's eligibility for primary credit at the Fed's discount window, and regulators can use a poor rating to deny approval for mergers and acquisitions.[296] The FDIC deposit insurance assessment also depends, in part, on the composite CAMELS rating and a weighted average of the component ratings.[297] Separately, a holding company cannot engage in expanded financial activities (beyond banking) unless its subsidiary depository institutions all remain "well-managed," a term that includes a composite CAMELS rating of 1 or 2, and at least a satisfactory rating for management.[298] The capital component rating—as well as, more broadly, the capital adequacy of the bank—can also trigger multiple regulatory restrictions on a bank's ability to operate, ranging from explicit constraints on funding sources and asset size to prohibitions on appointing new officers and directors.[299]

- **Capital requirements and regulation.** Federal banking agencies have the discretion to define what constitutes adequate capital levels. Each appropriate federal banking agency must establish minimum levels of capital for banks, and the statutory law provides regulators wide discretion to accomplish this task.[300] For instance, federal agencies can regulate banks' capital levels by using "such other methods as the appropriate Federal banking agency deems appropriate."[301] The law explicitly gives regulators the authority to determine adequate capital levels they judge "to be necessary or appropriate in light of the particular circumstances of the banking institution."[302] Currently, the federal banking agencies use the Basel III risk-weighted capital rules as their guidelines for banks' capital requirements.[303] Still, the Fed has wide discretion within that structure, including, on a case-by-case basis, to "assign a different risk-weighted asset amount to the exposure(s) or to deduct the amount of the exposure(s) from its regulatory capital."[304] The Fed also has the authority to apply capital-planning and stress-testing requirements to any top-tier bank holding company with total assets of at least $100 billion, and to apply capital adequacy requirements to any state member bank and US bank holding company.[305] For all banks, the failure to maintain adequate capital levels may "be deemed by the appropriate Federal banking agency, in its discretion, to constitute an unsafe and unsound practice," ultimately terminating a bank's ability to provide customers with FDIC deposit insurance—effectively a death sentence for a commercial bank operating in the United States.[306]
- **Reputational risk.** Starting in the 1990s, federal banking agencies began to identify "reputational risk" as part of their broader efforts to manage financial institutions' overall risks.[307]

Since that time, most federal agencies have clarified their views on reputational risks, and both the FDIC and the OCC have justified forcing banks to change their operating behavior on the basis of concerns over reputational risk.[308] According to the OCC, "Reputation risk is the risk to current or projected financial condition and resilience arising from negative public opinion," and "Reputation risk is inherent in all bank activities."[309] Moreover, OCC examiners now consider a bank's "quantity of reputation risk and quality of reputation risk management."[310] These risks include many different factors, ranging from the "types of third-party relationships" and the "types of assets" that are under management to the "market's or public's perception of the quality of the bank's products" and the "market's or public's perception of the bank's financial stability."[311] The Fed's official guidance defines "reputational risk" as "the potential that negative publicity regarding an institution's business practices, *whether true or not*, will cause a decline in the customer base, costly litigation, or revenue reductions."[312] The FDIC has not been as explicit in defining reputational risks, but its examination manual notes, among other things, that an institution's "reputation can be damaged from noncompliance with consumer protection laws."[313] Regardless, as discussed in chapter 7, both the OCC and the FDIC have forced banks to close customer accounts because of concerns over reputational risks.[314]

- **Unsafe or unsound practices.** The FDIC has an enormous amount of leverage over financial institutions because it can terminate a bank's status as an *insured* depository institution if it finds that the bank has engaged in or is "engaging in unsafe or unsound practices in conducting the business of such depository institution."[315] The FDIC, like the other federal banking regulators, is responsible for determining what constitutes unsafe or unsound practices. The law gives federal regulators "the authority to place limitations on the activities or functions of an insured depository institution or any institution-affiliated party."[316] When regulators determine that an insured depository institution has engaged in, or is about to engage in, an unsafe or unsound practice, they can issue a "cease and desist" order.[317]

- **Lending limits.** Federal law limits how much money a bank can lend to any one customer or to a group of related customers.[318] For loans and extensions of credit that are not fully secured with collateral, the total "to a person outstanding at one time" may not exceed 15 percent "of the unimpaired capital and unimpaired surplus" of the bank.[319] For those that are fully secured, the total cannot exceed 10 percent, but this restriction is "separate from and in addition to" the limitation on loans that are not fully secured.[320] Still, federal regulators have the authority to promulgate rules and regulations for these lending limits for national banks, including "rules or regulations to define or further define terms used in this section [of the law]," as well as "to establish limits or requirements *other than those specified in this section* [of the law] for particular classes or categories of loans or extensions of credit."[321]

- **Special discretion through Dodd-Frank.** The Dodd-Frank Act expanded regulators' discretion in both the banking and nonbanking segments. For example, Dodd-Frank authorizes the Fed to develop prudential regulatory standards for the *nonbank* financial firms they supervise, explicitly "to prevent or mitigate risks to the financial stability of the United States that could arise from the material financial distress or failure, or ongoing activities, of large, interconnected financial institutions."[322] The law does not, however, define "financial stability."

OVERVIEW OF MAJOR LEGISLATIVE CHANGES TO BANK REGULATION

As the banking industry evolved during the post–World War II period, Congress passed many laws that shaped the regulatory framework. It would be impossible to provide a comprehensive description of all these banking laws in this book, so this section provides a brief discussion of several core changes and a list of the most important laws that form the overall regulatory framework.

There is, perhaps, no better example of a crisis driving popular support for regulatory reforms than the changes Congress made during the Great Depression. After a major market crash in 1929 and a wave of bank failures that peaked in 1933, Congress made historic changes that still influence the financial regulatory framework. For instance, Congress passed the Securities Act of 1933 and the Securities Exchange Act of 1934, both of which still form the basis of America's securities law framework. And while the Banking Act of 1933, better known as the Glass–Steagall Act, is known for creating a legal separation between commercial banks and investment banks, it also created the Federal Deposit Insurance Corporation and implemented several other major changes.[323]

For instance, Section 17 of the Glass–Steagall Act created a minimum capital requirement for national banks that was tied to population. It required a minimum of $50,000 in areas with fewer than 6,000 people, $100,000 in areas with a population of up to 50,000, and $200,000 in areas that exceeded 50,000 people. Section 21 instituted a requirement for banks to submit to periodic examinations by the comptroller of the currency or the Federal Reserve, and for each bank to publish reports of its financial condition that exhibited "in detail its resources and liabilities." Section 22 gave national banks the ability to become limited liability corporations, essentially removing double liability for their shareholders (shareholders of a failed bank lost the value of their shares *and* were responsible for paying an amount equal to their original investment). And Section 31 required boards of directors for all national banks and Fed-member banks to consist of between 5 and 25 members, with each director owning shares worth no less than $2,500.

In 1966, Congress greatly expanded federal regulators' discretion in a way that has remained integral to federal banking regulation. Specifically, the Financial Institutions Supervisory Act allowed regulators to bring "cease and desist orders" against banks engaged in "unsafe and unsound banking practices."[324] The act also increased FDIC insurance coverage to $15,000, and gave federal regulators the authority to terminate a bank's FDIC insurance and to remove a bank's officers and directors for engaging in unsafe or unsound practices. No crisis precipitated this legislation, but federal banking agencies explicitly asked Congress for this additional authority so that they could better address problems facing them in their supervisory functions.[325]

In the 1980s and 1990s, the savings and loan crisis helped advance two major pieces of legislation. The first was the Financial Institutions Reform, Recovery, and Enforcement Act of 1989 (FIRREA), which abolished the Federal Home Loan Bank Board (the regulator for the Federal Home Loan Bank System created during the Depression) and the Federal Savings and Loan Insurance Corporation (FSLIC), the equivalent of the FDIC for savings and loan institutions. The FIRREA also gave the FDIC the initial responsibility for managing the Resolution Trust Corporation, a temporary federal agency created to resolve the failed savings and loan institutions.[326]

Then in 1991, Congress passed the Federal Deposit Insurance Corporation Improvement Act of 1991 (FDICIA), a major piece of legislation that changed the FDIC's bank resolution powers and gave regulators more discretion. Section 111 of the FDICIA required federal regulators to conduct a "full-scope, on-site examination" for most banks at least once every 12 months, and Section 131 created a system of "prompt corrective action" that remains a key part of US banking law.[327]

Essentially, the prompt corrective action framework requires federal banking regulators to take progressively severe action to "correct" the situation when a bank's capital position deteriorates. To implement this framework, the FDICIA requires regulators to assign banks to one of five capital categories: (a) well capitalized, (b) adequately capitalized, (c) undercapitalized, (d) significantly undercapitalized, or (e) critically undercapitalized. When a bank falls into the critically undercapitalized category, the FDICIA, with some exceptions, requires the bank to be placed into conservatorship or receivership.[328] Although the FDICIA gave federal banking regulators the discretion to develop various capital requirements, it mandated some components of those requirements, such as a leverage limit and a risk-based capital requirement.

Throughout the post–World War II period, Congress has used many other laws to shape the financial regulatory framework, especially in the banking sector. Figure 5.1 briefly describes the most important of those laws.

Figure 5.1: Timeline of laws that shaped the banking sector

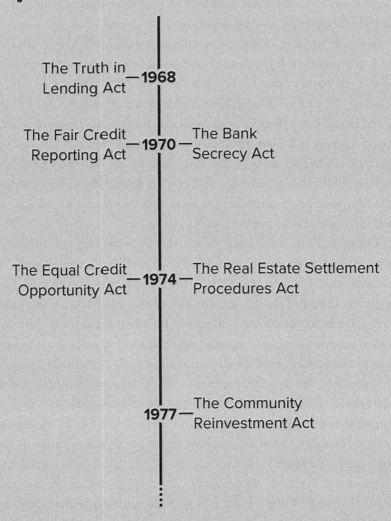

The Truth in Lending Act of 1968 (TILA)

The TILA, also known as the Consumer Credit Protection Act, requires various disclosures about the terms and conditions of loans, providing a generally standardized set of procedures for calculating borrowing costs and disclosing them to consumers. The TILA also regulates certain practices in the credit card market and provides a regulatory framework for resolving credit billing disputes.

The Fair Credit Reporting Act of 1970 (FCRA)

The FCRA regulates the personal information that goes into consumers' files as compiled by credit reporting agencies. It also regulates consumers' access to credit reports and procedures for ensuring accuracy and privacy.

The Bank Secrecy Act of 1970 (BSA)

The BSA and its later amendments, including the Uniting and Strengthening America by Providing Appropriate Tools Required to Intercept and Obstruct Terrorism (USA PATRIOT) Act in 2001, require financial institutions in the United States to assist government agencies in detecting and preventing money laundering and other crimes. The BSA now forms the basis of the federal anti-money laundering (AML) and know-your-customer (KYC) rules and regulations, an extensive, intrusive, and costly regulatory framework.

The Equal Credit Opportunity Act of 1974 (ECOA)

The ECOA prohibits discriminatory lending practices for various protected classes, including those based on race, color, religion, national origin, sex or marital status, or age (provided the applicant has the capacity to contract).

The Real Estate Settlement Procedures Act of 1974 (RESPA)

The RESPA governs real estate settlement processes throughout the United States. The law requires lenders, mortgage brokers, and servicers to provide borrowers with certain disclosures regarding the terms and costs of the settlement process for real estate transactions.

The Community Reinvestment Act of 1977 (CRA)

The original intent of the CRA was to encourage banks to meet the needs of borrowers in the same communities where their deposit base is located. The law was passed to reduce alleged discriminatory lending practices in low-income neighborhoods. Federal banking regulators enforce this law by considering banks' CRA compliance when approving applications for mergers, acquisitions, or new branches.

(continued)

Figure 5.1 *(continued)*

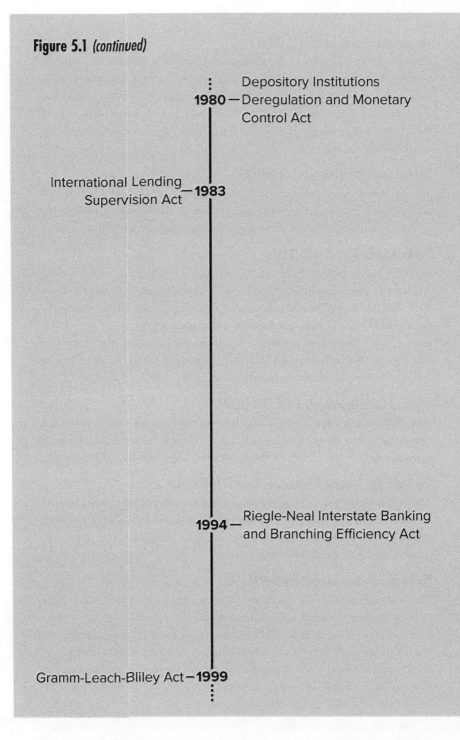

Depository Institutions Deregulation and Monetary Control Act of 1980

This law was referred to as deregulatory because it began a six-year phase-out of a price control on the interest rates that banks were allowed to pay depositors (known as Regulation Q, a price control in place since the 1930s). The price control was lifted largely out of necessity because market interest rates were so high, and rising so rapidly, that people were moving their money out of banks and into capital markets (a process known as disintermediation). Section 303 of the law created a new interest-bearing account that banks could provide (known as negotiable order of withdrawal, or NOW, accounts), and Section 308 raised the FDIC deposit coverage ceiling from $40,000 to $100,000. Just as important, Title I of the law required all depository institutions to hold reserves at the Fed. Before 1980, only commercial banks that were members of the Fed were subject to the Fed's reserve requirements, and only 40 percent of commercial banks were members of the Fed.

International Lending Supervision Act of 1983

This law required federal banking regulators to evaluate the foreign country exposure and transfer risk of banks, but it also required regulators to set minimum capital adequacy standards, and to define what constitutes adequate capital levels. It was the precursor to the United States' joining efforts to standardize bank capital requirements through the Basel Accords.

Riegle-Neal Interstate Banking and Branching Effciency Act of 1994

This law phased in the formal allowance of interstate mergers for commercial banks, provided they were adequately capitalized and managed. Merger approval rests with the Fed, and mergers and acquisitions remain subject to market concentration limits, state laws, and (vaguely defined) CRA requirements.

Gramm-Leach-Bliley Act of 1999 (GLBA)

The GLBA repealed the Glass-Steagall Act's Sections 20 and 32, which generally prohibited commercial banks from affiliating with investment banks. That is, the law authorized banks to affiliate with companies engaged in securities underwriting or dealing. It amended the Bank Holding Company Act of 1956 to give the Federal Reserve the responsibility of regulating all bank holding companies and to allow banks and insurance underwriters to affiliate with one another.

(continued)

Figure 5.1 *(continued)*

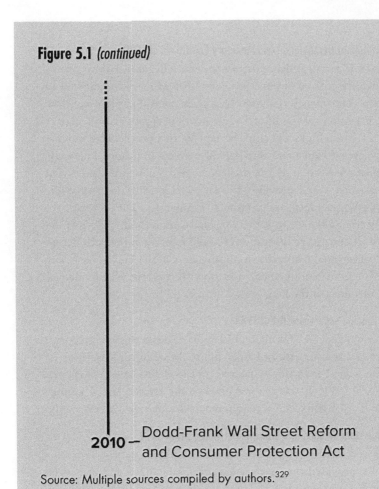

2010 — Dodd-Frank Wall Street Reform and Consumer Protection Act

Source: Multiple sources compiled by authors.[329]

Dodd-Frank Wall Street Reform and Consumer Protection Act of 2010

The Dodd-Frank Act was the congressional response to the 2008 financial crisis, and it implemented many changes to the regulatory framework. Title X created a new federal agency, the Consumer Financial Protection Bureau, and Title I created the Financial Stability Oversight Council (FSOC), which has the authority to designate nonbank financial companies for prudential regulations. The law gave federal banking regulators new discretionary powers—including new bank resolution powers and heightened capital requirements—covering so-called systemically important financial institutions, or SIFIs. It also made changes to the way derivatives are regulated and mortgages are underwritten, and it broadly increased federal mandates to regulate based on maintaining financial stability, though it does not define financial stability.

The laws listed in figure 5.1 only scratch the surface of the incredibly complex bank regulatory framework.[330] The core of US banking law, which is in Title 12 of the *United States Code* (Banks and Banking), includes 55 chapters. Moreover, the volume of rules to codify these laws is enormous—the US Code of Federal Regulations for Title 12 consists of 18 chapters, with 1,815 parts.[331]

As mentioned earlier, regulators have extensively managed banks' activities for many decades, especially after Congress created the FDIC. Throughout the post–World War II era, banking regulations have increasingly focused on risk management conducted by regulatory agencies, with much of this regulation justified as necessary for protecting the FDIC's Deposit Insurance Fund. In addition to protecting taxpayers, who are ultimately responsible for all FDIC-insured losses, bank regulations have also increasingly been justified by citing systemic-risk concerns. Increasingly, systemic-risk concerns have also been used to justify securities regulation. Moreover, although large differences remain between banking and securities regulation, federal regulators have increasingly taken on a more active role in managing nonbank financial firms' activities as well. The next section provides an overview of the regulatory framework for securities markets.

OVERVIEW OF SECURITIES MARKETS REGULATION

Securities markets are generally regulated differently from the banking sector. Rather than prudential regulation, securities market regulation is traditionally described as disclosure-based regulation intended to alleviate information asymmetries between the purchasers and sellers of securities.[332] But this description oversimplifies the securities regulatory framework, which in practice goes far beyond attempting to level the informational playing field.

The Securities and Exchange Commission is tasked with the regulation of securities on the federal level, and it receives its authority through a series of statutes, largely enacted between 1933 and 1940, that regulate the conduct of particular participants in the securities markets: issuers of securities, those engaged in the secondary-market sales of securities, and those engaged in managing the investment of securities.

Since the beginning of modern securities regulation, however, it has long been clear that the characterization of such regulation as "disclosure-based" does not tell the whole story.[333] For instance, the Securities Exchange Act of 1934 introduced a net capital rule for broker-dealers that dictated the type and amount of liquid assets that broker-dealers had to maintain.[334] The rule has been amended several times, including a major adjustment in 1975 after a series of firm failures in the late 1960s and early 1970s, and again in 2004—just a few years before the 2008 financial crisis—becoming more prescriptive each time.[335]

Although the securities regulatory landscape is not as complex as that for banking, those involved in the securities markets may also be subject to a number of different regulators, depending on the exact function in which the market participant is engaging, including (a) the Securities and Exchange Commission; (b) the Commodity Futures Trading Commission; (c) the Financial Industry Regulatory Authority; (d) other self-regulatory organizations, such as the New York Stock Exchange or other exchanges or the National Futures Association; (e) the Financial Crimes Enforcement Network, a bureau of the Treasury Department; and (f) state-level regulators, including securities-specific regulators.

Because the contours of securities regulation often depend on the role that an individual or entity is playing in the market, it is useful to break down regulation by the type of market participant. Many financial entities engage in multiple lines of business that would make them subject to multiple types of securities regulation.[336]

SECURITIES ISSUERS

Federal securities laws impose a host of disclosure obligations on companies that wish to sell securities to the public. Instead of requiring offerings to be approved by the SEC as "fair, just, and equitable to the investor," as many state-level "merit review" regimes require, the Securities Act of 1933 requires that issuers provide certain disclosures to the public as part of registering an offering for public sale. Those disclosures occur (a) when the offering is initially made through the offering's registration statement (Form S-1) and, for many securities trading in the secondary market, (b) on a regular basis thereafter. Ongoing disclosure, as required by the Securities Exchange Act of 1934 and implementing regulations, currently takes the form of annual (Form 10-K) and quarterly reports (Form 10-Q), as well as special reporting triggered by the occurrence of certain events (Form 8-K).[337]

Offerings are essentially presumed to be public, and thus requiring registration, unless they can demonstrate that they meet an exemption from registration. Such exempt offerings, however, are not free from all obligations under the securities laws. They not only remain subject to the securities law prohibitions against false and misleading statements, but also may be required to meet certain disclosure or other requirements in order to satisfy the conditions of the exemption.[338]

The scope of required disclosures has long been understood to encompass information necessary for investors to value securities, primarily a company's financial performance and information about its business. These disclosures are also generally limited to "material" information, which the Supreme Court, in a 1976 case, defined as information for which there exists "a substantial likelihood that the disclosure . . . would have been viewed by the reasonable investor as having significantly altered the 'total mix' of information made available."[339]

Over time, the volume and complexity of required disclosure have grown. And at times, required disclosures have served as vehicles to promote policy goals unrelated to their original purpose. For example, the 2010 Dodd-Frank Act required public companies to disclose whether certain minerals used in their products were sourced from specific geographic areas because of concerns that trade in those minerals helped finance armed conflict in the Democratic Republic of the Congo, threatening to worsen the humanitarian crisis there.[340] In this case and others, disclosure requirements are intended to change the behavior of the company making the disclosure, which demonstrates the sway that a "disclosure-focused" regime can have on underlying issuer behavior. Even when the regulation is not designed to change issuer behavior, expansive SEC disclosure rules often have unintended effects on the conduct of the regulated party. Unsurprisingly, research suggests that the burden of public company disclosures plays a role in a company's decision to go public and may be one factor in the decline in the number of public companies since the 1990s.[341]

The SEC enforces compliance with rules applicable to issuers in two ways.[342] The first is through enforcement actions. The agency investigates suspected violations, and issuers that fail to comply with regulatory requirements are subject to penalties. The other way the SEC enforces compliance is through preemptive review of certain disclosures. For example, the SEC reviews registration statements before it permits them to become effective. This review—replete with the agency's exercise of discretion to find "deficiencies" that the issuer is required to correct before being allowed to offer the securities—is another process that chips away at the fiction that securities regulation is merely concerned with disclosure.[343]

BROKERS AND DEALERS

Under the Securities Exchange Act, the SEC has the authority to register, regulate, and discipline broker-dealers and regulate securities exchanges, along with their self-regulatory organizations. Today, at the national level, broker-dealers are subject to regulation by the SEC and the Financial Industry Regulatory Authority (FINRA)—a self-regulatory organization—as well as any exchanges for which the broker-dealer is a member (also self-regulatory organizations). Broker-dealers are required to register with the SEC and a self-regulatory organization in order to conduct business.[344]

Registration subjects a broker-dealer to conduct regulation, which governs how a broker-dealer interacts with its customers and executes trades. Such regulation is sometimes referred to as being disclosure based because it governs the disclosure of information to customers, but broker-dealer regulation is far more prescriptive than a disclosure-based regime. In fact, even the standard of care that brokers owe their customers—which is at the very heart of a disclosure-based relationship between the customer and broker—has become more restrictive over time. The standard previously required that a broker make a "suitable" recommendation for a customer. But in 2019, the SEC implemented a new rule requiring brokers to use a new standard of care that permits only recommendations made in the "best interest" of the customer.[345] And although the adoption of this new standard also came with a new set of disclosures that must be made to a customer (Form CRS), it is difficult to consider this conduct rule as being disclosure based, since it restricts the advice that a broker may provide.

Moreover, self-regulatory organizations (including stock exchanges) and SEC rules dictate many broker-dealer operations with precision: how trades are to be reported, what records are to be kept by the broker-dealer, how customer funds are to be managed, what information can be shared among different business lines at a broker-dealer, how credit can be extended to customers, how brokers and customers may use electronic signatures, and so on. Some of this regulation is aimed at mitigating risks that individual investors face when using a broker—that is, the risk of bad advice or the risk that a broker loses the customer's money. But some of this regulation—such as the net capital rule—is more ambiguous in that it seeks to protect both an individual customer from the risk of a firm's failure and the firm from failing in the first place.[346] The SEC has specifically characterized regulation aimed at enhancing operational integrity and limiting abrupt market movements in individual securities as aimed at reducing "systemic risk" in the securities markets.[347]

Broker-dealers are subject to examination by their regulators. The SEC conducts limited broker-dealer examinations, but FINRA has an extensive examination program, overseen by the SEC, that regularly reviews the operations of registered broker-dealers. Similar to bank examiners, securities regulators exercise a great deal of discretion during the examination process, making suggestions about a broker-dealer's operations, as well as deciding whether potential violations rise to a level of further investigation by the self-regulatory organization's or the SEC's enforcement divisions.[348]

INVESTMENT ADVISERS

The Investment Advisers Act of 1940 gives the SEC the authority to regulate individuals or entities that are engaged in the business of providing investment advice to clients or issuing reports or analyses regarding securities.[349] This authority covers money managers, investment consultants, financial planners, and others who may have different titles but

provide similar services. All investment advisers are subject to the legislation's prohibitions on fraud, but only certain investment advisers must
register with the SEC. The contours of which advisers must register with
the SEC have changed over time, changing the allocation of responsibility of investment adviser regulation between the states and the SEC.
Currently, advisers with less than $100 million in assets under manage-
ment are subject to state regulation, whereas advisers with more than
$100 million in assets under management or those who advise registered
investment companies are subject to SEC regulation.[350]

The SEC describes the investment adviser regulatory regime as one
of disclosure, noting that the law is not prescriptive, but "rather, investors have the responsibility, based on the disclosure they receive, for
selecting their own advisers, negotiating their own fee arrangements,
and evaluating their advisers' conflicts."[351] But again, this characterization understates the degree to which the SEC's regulation limits and
directs adviser conduct.

One of the fundamental tenets of Advisers Act regulation is the
notion that advisers act as fiduciaries to their clients. The Supreme
Court describes the act as reflecting a "congressional recognition of the
delegate fiduciary nature of an investment advisory relationship as well
as a congressional intent to eliminate, or at least expose, all conflicts
of interest which might incline an investment adviser—consciously or
unconsciously—to render advice which was not disinterested."[352] This
requires disclosure of facts about a conflict of interest so that a client can
decide whether to enter into an advisory relationship with the adviser.
The SEC, however, also prohibits advisers from undertaking certain
activities that the SEC views as placing the fiduciary relationship at risk
or potentially running afoul of anti-fraud provisions.[353] The SEC also
regulates certain aspects of advisers' contracts with their clients.

These rules go well beyond disclosure, and as with broker-dealer
regulation, the SEC has increasingly expanded its responsibilities for
investment adviser regulation to include safeguarding against systemic
risk. For example, Title IV of the Dodd-Frank Act requires the SEC to
establish reporting requirements for investment advisers to private funds.
Private fund advisers who manage more than $150 million are required
to report information about the funds that they advise on Form PF,

which was recently updated to require more detailed information about the strategies followed and investments made by the funds they advise. Those details are intended to "enhance the [SEC and CFTC's] and FSOC's understanding of the private fund industry as well as the potential systemic risk posed by the industry and its individual participants."[354]

Like broker-dealers, investment advisers are also subject to examination by the regulator. Currently, the SEC examines annually about 15 percent of the 15,000 advisers who are registered with the agency.[355] In addition to the discretion inherent in the examination process, with respect to broker-dealers, the SEC's method of selecting which advisers are subject to examination is an exercise in discretion, with the SEC using a "dynamic" "risk-based" approach to determining which advisers will be examined and on which areas the examination will focus.[356]

INVESTMENT COMPANIES

The Investment Company Act of 1940 provides the primary regulatory framework for the regulation of investment companies. Investment companies include mutual funds, closed-end funds, unit investment trusts, and exchange traded funds.[357]

The Investment Company Act requires all investment companies to register with the SEC (unless subject to an exemption, as described in chapter 3), and it regulates their conduct through a combination of disclosure requirements and prescriptions and prohibitions about the company's operations. Disclosure includes both the fund's prospectus, which must remain updated, and periodic reports to shareholders on financial performance and how a fund has voted on specific proxy issues in the companies in which it is invested. Funds must also provide detailed information to the SEC (some of which is made publicly available) about the fund's holdings and transactions (Form N-PORT). However, the operation of investment companies is also heavily affected by the regulation of investment advisers and brokers—which an investment company uses—and issuers—which include investment companies.

The story is familiar: although disclosure is often referred to as the backbone of this type of regulation, the reality is that the regulatory requirements go much further in shaping an investment company. For example, the Investment Company Act requires that a certain percentage of a fund's board be independent, prohibits the use of complex capital structures by funds, limits funds' use of leverage, and prohibits transactions between the fund and affiliates.

This regulation is generally characterized as addressing risks to investors, but the SEC has at times characterized it as supporting the minimization of "systemic" risk.[358] And outside the SEC, the FSOC recently proposed changes to the process for designating nonbanks as "systemically important financial institutions," with the process largely expected to focus on whether major asset managers should be subject to US Federal Reserve oversight and heightened capital and liquidity requirements.[359]

Like broker-dealers and investment advisers, investment companies are subject to examination. The examination process entails high degrees of regulatory discretion granted to the SEC to shape the conduct of an investment company before the finding of any violation of an existing law or rule.[360]

DERIVATIVES REGULATION

In most cases, the regulation of derivatives is covered by a separate set of laws and a separate regulator, the Commodity Futures Trading Commission. The SEC, however, maintains jurisdiction over securities derivatives, and the SEC and CFTC share authority over a small class of other derivatives.

The CFTC was created in 1974 as an independent agency with more authority than its predecessor, the Commodity Exchange Authority, which only regulated futures trading in certain agricultural commodities.[361] This overhaul laid the foundation for modern derivatives regulation that covers a wider range of contracts concerning agricultural, financial, and other assets. Self-regulatory organizations also play a role in derivatives regulation; as in securities markets, derivatives exchanges generally operate as self-regulatory organizations and the National Futures Association is the self-regulatory organization for off-exchange conduct. Market participants—futures commission merchants,

commodity trading advisers, commodity pool operators, floor participants, brokers, and so on—must register with both the CFTC and the
relevant self-regulatory organization.

The Commodity Exchange Act, which was passed in 1936 and has
been amended several times since, gives the CFTC the authority to regulate futures and options on commodities. Almost anything can be a
commodity under the act. Title VII of the Dodd-Frank Act also created
a framework for the regulation of over-the-counter (OTC) swaps markets, which creates a shared responsibility for regulation between the
SEC and CFTC.

The focus on regulation in the derivatives markets is on the contract itself and on the trading of that contract. Whereas the CFTC has
some authority to police fraud in an underlying asset to a contract if the
fraud affects the price of the derivative, the CFTC's primary authority
relates to the trading of the contract. To that end, the CFTC regulates trading platforms, clearinghouses, and intermediaries. Investors
are provided with considerably less specific disclosure about a contract
than about an investment in a stock or investment fund, but retail
investors in futures and options contracts are required to receive general disclosure about the risks, features, and costs associated with those
types of contracts.

The CFTC is responsible for approving contracts offered on exchanges;
this is generally done by approving a contract type or changes to a contract
type, rather than approving each individual contract.[362] The evaluation
process hinges on the regulator's discretion: a new contract has to comply
with existing market rules, but the CFTC also considers whether the contract has appropriate risk management in place and, importantly, whether
it serves some economic purpose and is in the public interest.[363]

The CFTC also maintains rules regarding net capital, risk management, and record-keeping and engages in market surveillance to
prevent abusive trading practices, market manipulation, and disruptions
to market integrity.

The Dodd-Frank Act significantly expanded the CFTC's authority
over derivatives markets, including oversight of swaps and broader
authority to set position limits to prevent excessive speculation and

manipulation.[364] Oversight and regulation of the OTC derivatives market was a dramatic expansion of the CFTC's regulatory authority, including requiring the registration and oversight of swap dealers and market participants, centralized clearing requirements, rules governing the operation of trading platforms, and position limits.[365] These changes were enacted specifically to combat "systemic risk" within the financial system in the wake of the 2008 financial crisis.

Although the CFTC examines futures and options market participants, it does not have an examination program with respect to swap execution facilities.

OVERVIEW OF MAJOR LEGISLATIVE CHANGES TO SECURITIES REGULATION

The fundamentals of securities regulation remain underpinned by a quartet of statutes passed during the Great Depression: the Securities Act of 1933, the Securities Exchange Act of 1934, the Investment Company Act of 1940, and the Investment Advisers Act of 1940. Figure 5.2 briefly describes these laws and the most important other legislative actions that shape securities and derivatives market regulation today.

Figure 5.2, of course, does not provide a full picture of legislative actions relating to securities and derivatives regulation, and it omits legislative actions that affect private securities litigation (most of which is based on the violations of laws that the SEC also enforces). Just as importantly, the figure does not reflect the significant impact of administrative rulemaking on the regulation of securities and derivatives markets, as the statutes that underpin the regulation of these markets impart significant discretion to the regulators to promulgate rules.

INCREASED REGULATION HASN'T INCREASED STABILITY

All the increased regulation during the past 100-plus years has not delivered on protecting taxpayers or keeping financial markets stable. Although many still fear that private markets must be heavily regulated to create stability and prevent financial crises, the evidence doesn't support such a view.

Figure 5.2: Timeline of laws that shaped the securities and derivatives markets

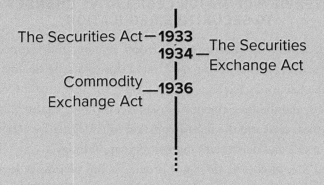

The Securities Act of 1933

The Securities Act governs primary offerings of securities. It requires every offer of securities to be registered with the SEC (unless it has an applicable exemption from registration). This act, and rules promulgated pursuant to it, require an issuer of securities to file a registration statement that discloses information about the securities to be offered for sale and management of the issuer, as well as the issuer's audited financial statements. The Securities Act also establishes strict liability for any misstatements in the registration statement, requiring a high degree of due diligence, to avoid liability, both by the issuer and by those assisting with the offering, such as underwriters and accountants.

The Securities Exchange Act of 1934

The Exchange Act governs the secondary trading of securities. In addition to creating the Securities and Exchange Commission, the Exchange Act required the registration of brokers and dealers, whether or not they are members of a securities exchange, and forms the basis for broker-dealer regulation. The Exchange Act and its implementing regulations also require periodic disclosure from publicly traded companies, including information about the company's finances and management. The most well-known anti-fraud provision in the securities laws, Section 10(b), is also a part of the Exchange Act, and prohibits a wide variety of conduct that can be understood as a "manipulative or deceptive device or contrivance" in connection with the purchase or sale of a security.

Commodity Exchange Act

The Commodity Exchange Act (CEA) was passed in 1936. This was not the first federal act regulating futures trading, but it is the one that forms the basis for modern derivatives regulation. The CEA expanded federal regulation to a much larger group of commodities futures than previously and granted the Commodity Exchange Commission, a predecessor to the modern CFTC that consisted of the secretary of agriculture, secretary of commerce, and attorney general, the authority to establish speculative position limits. The CEA was amended multiple times in subsequent years to add to the list of regulated commodities.

(continued)

Figure 5.2 *(continued)*

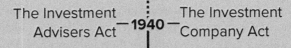

The Investment Advisers Act —1940— The Investment Company Act

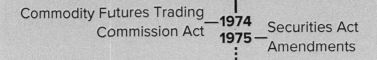

Commodity Futures Trading Commission Act —1974— 1975— Securities Act Amendments

The Investment Advisers Act of 1940

The Investment Advisers Act regulates the activities of those who provide investment advice for a fee. The Advisers Act initially required that all individuals and entities providing investment advice on an interstate basis to register with the SEC, although those provisions have changed over the years. Currently, only advisers who have at least $100 million of assets under management or advise a registered investment company must register with the SEC. The Advisers Act, and rules promulgated pursuant to it, govern the operations of investment advisers, including adviser advertising, control of client assets, and information disclosure.

The Investment Company Act of 1940

The Investment Company Act regulates investment funds, including mutual funds, closed-end funds, and exchange-traded funds. Along with regulations promulgated pursuant to it, the Investment Company Act requires disclosures from funds to investors about the fund's financial condition and investments, as well as places restrictions on certain fund activities and mandates certain aspects of a fund's corporate structure and operations.

Commodity Futures Trading Commission Act of 1974

This act created the Commodity Futures Trading Commission, an independent agency with greater powers than its predecessors. The CFTC's jurisdiction also extended to futures trading in all commodities, not just agricultural ones.

Securities Act Amendments of 1975

In 1975, the Securities Act and the Exchange Act were amended to foster the development of a national securities market and a national clearance and settlement system for securities. The SEC implemented this legislation through a number of regulations (which are now consolidated into Regulation NMS) that govern stock price quotations and trade executions across trading platforms, among other things. These amendments were intended to encourage competition for investors across what was a fragmented marketplace, but the rules that have followed from these amendments marked a shift from a more limited role for the SEC in enforcing general duties and obligations of market participants to managing the specifics of how the market should execute trades.

(continued)

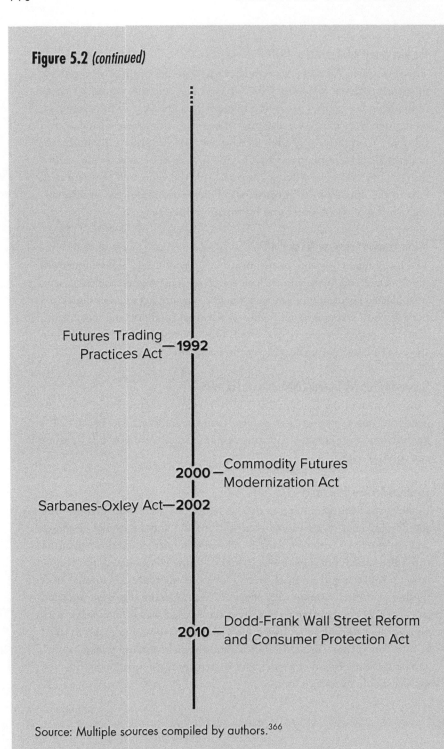

Figure 5.2 *(continued)*

Futures Trading Practices Act—**1992**

2000—Commodity Futures Modernization Act

Sarbanes-Oxley Act—**2002**

2010—Dodd-Frank Wall Street Reform and Consumer Protection Act

Source: Multiple sources compiled by authors.[366]

Futures Trading Practices Act of 1992

The Futures Trading Practices Act gave the CFTC authority to exempt OTC derivative and other transactions from CFTC regulation. Before this act, however, the CFTC had already exercised authority to exclude certain products, including certain swap transactions, from CFTC regulation based on the CFTC's finding that the products were not futures. The Futures Trading Practices Act clarified this authority and allowed the CFTC to exempt specific products from regulation without having to determine that those products were not futures. Shortly thereafter, in 1993, the CFTC issued a series of exemptions for swaps, hybrid instruments, contracts for deferred purchase, or sale of certain energy products.

Commodity Futures Modernization Act of 2000

The CFMA enshrined in legislation many of the exemptions of OTC derivatives, including swaps, from regulation under the Commodity Exchange Act. (Banks' use of such derivatives, however, remained subject to supervision by banking regulators.)

Sarbanes-Oxley Act of 2002

The Sarbanes-Oxley Act, also known as the Public Company Accounting Reform and Investor Protection Act and the Corporate and Auditing Accountability, Responsibility, and Transparency Act, established the PCAOB (Public Company Accounting Oversight Board) and required a number of standards with regard to financial auditing, corporate responsibility for financial reporting, and financial disclosures required of public companies.

Dodd-Frank Wall Street Reform and Consumer Protection Act of 2010

As previously described, the Dodd-Frank Act was the congressional response to the 2008 financial crisis, and it implemented many changes to the regulatory framework. In addition to creating the Financial Stability Oversight Council, which has the authority to designate nonbank financial companies as being subject to prudential regulations, Title VII imposes a requirement to clear more OTC derivatives through swap execution facilities and gives the CFTC and the SEC explicit authority to regulate the OTC swaps markets and market participants. The Dodd-Frank Act also updated thresholds for SEC regulation of investment advisers, requiring advisers to register with the SEC if they have more than $100 million in assets under management, or advise registered investment companies, and removing an exemption for registration that applied to advisers for private funds. The act also requires private fund advisers to report information about the funds they advise for review by the SEC, CFTC, and FSOC.

For instance, historical experience shows that banking is not inherently unstable, and that most historical American banking crises can be traced to ill-conceived regulations and legal restrictions.[367] Moreover, although the United States has steadily increased regulation across financial sectors, it has one of the worst track records of all developed nations regarding financial crises.

For example, there were 14 banking crises in the United States between 1837 and 2009, versus only 2—mild ones—in Canada.[368] Separately, among severe economic contractions in six developed nations from 1870 to 1933, banking crises occurred only in the United States.[369] These problems are not concentrated in the distant past—the United States is one of only three developed countries with at least two banking crises between 1970 and 2010.[370]

Additionally, it is incredibly difficult to find historical examples of contagion—when a panic spreads like an infectious disease to otherwise healthy banks—that threatened the entire financial system.[371] In fact, the evidence demonstrates that this story is highly flawed. For starters, in all the well-studied banking panics between 1793 and 1933, among the United States, England, France, and Germany, only the 1933 crisis in the United States appears to have consisted of a truly system-wide panic.[372] Moreover, even though many US banks failed in the 1920s and early 1930s, widespread panic was not a feature of the American crisis until February 1933, and that crisis was not sparked by a run on a single bank that turned into a panic. Instead, the 1933 panic was provoked mainly by the federal government's plan to devalue the US dollar, not any inherent weakness in the financial system.[373] Moreover, although contagion in the so-called shadow banking sector is often blamed for panicked "runs" during the 2008 financial crisis, the evidence suggests that, instead of contagion, investors made carefully targeted moves to improve their financial positions, often due to regulatory or legal requirements.[374]

CONCLUSION

As we have argued in the preceding chapters, a well-functioning financial sector results in a society with more goods and services, more employment opportunities, and higher incomes. A smoothly running financial system makes it easier and less costly to raise the capital necessary for launching or operating a business, to borrow money for buying or building a home, and to invest in ideas that improve productivity and increase wealth. As we have also pointed out, when it comes to financial crises, US financial markets have one of the worst—if not the worst—track records in the developed world.

The basic idea behind regulation is that it will maintain financial stability and minimize the chances of financial crises occurring. Put differently, the regulatory framework is supposed to maximize people's ability to allocate capital and improve productivity as safely as possible. As this chapter has demonstrated, there is no doubt that the United States has a massive financial regulatory framework for banking and securities markets. Out of necessity, the chapter only scratches the surface. Complete books have been written about regulation in each sector, one for banking and another for securities.

This book does not provide a comprehensive history of regulation; however, it does mention some of the most notorious cases of regulation that caused—or contributed to—financial crises, both before and after the Great Depression. Despite these well-documented cases, and the fact that financial regulation has pretty much always been on an increasing trend in the United States, the conventional view rarely identifies too much regulation—or poorly designed regulatory policies—as a cause of financial crises. Curiously, the opposite view has dominated the public discourse, and deregulated financial markets generally receive the blame for financial crises. The next chapter debunks this deregulation story, particularly as it applies to the 2008 financial crisis.

Chapter 6
Correcting the Deregulation Myth of the 2008 Financial Crisis

In his best-selling book, *The Big Short: Inside the Doomsday Machine*, author Michael Lewis depicts the origins of the 2008 financial crisis as a series of events that took place outside the view of financial regulators.[375] Supposedly, only the geeky financial engineers of Wall Street really understood the risk of these impenetrable securities, designed to profit off the backs of low-income Americans who couldn't possibly repay their debts. The 2015 movie *The Big Short*, based on Lewis's book, essentially portrays the crisis in the same manner.

On a positive note, both the book and the movie provide excellent explanations of complex financial topics central to the crisis, including mortgage-backed securities (MBS), short selling, credit default swaps, and subprime loans. Still, they both had two major shortcomings. First, it is simply not true that regulators had no idea what was going on. Second, the book and movie largely gave federal officials a pass for any policies that might have contributed to the crisis.[376]

As previous chapters have demonstrated, political considerations have always shaped US regulatory policy, and American financial markets have been extensively regulated for decades. Even the asset securitization process itself, which started long before the 2008 crisis, has always been conducted in plain view of regulators. As discussed in chapter 2, nonbank financial firms involved in securitization have always worked closely with commercial banks, and federal regulators—especially federal *banking* regulators—had full knowledge of this relationship. In fact, from 1990 to 2008, commercial banks' market share for the principal functions of securitization was well over 90 percent.[377] This market share is sufficient reason to question the narrative that "deregulated" markets caused the crisis.

Perhaps most damaging for the conventional story—the one portrayed in *The Big Short*—is the historical track record of those supposedly impenetrable securities. Research from the University of Chicago shows, for instance, that the *low-risk* tranches of the private-label residential mortgage-backed securities performed relatively well, as expected. As economics professor Harald Uhlig shows, those AAA-rated securities issued between 1987 and 2013 experienced *cumulative* losses of "2.3 percent until December 2013, a loss rate that . . . is not necessarily small, but neither is it large enough to warrant the weight that many have put on these securities for the Financial Crisis."[378]

Additionally, the losses on the *non-investment-grade* bonds were much higher, pushing the loss rate for *all* private-label securities to 6.3 percent. This difference is problematic for the conventional story because higher losses for the higher-risk securities is exactly what should be expected from the securitization process.[379] Nobody purchasing the riskier securities could reasonably have been under the impression that those securities were safe, not in isolation or compared with the lower-risk tranches. They were, by definition, risky.

It is true that commercial banks experienced higher-than-expected losses from mortgage-backed securities, but those losses began mounting in 2007, not 2008, and federal regulators were clearly aware of these issues.[380] In fact, they were complicit. Long before 2007, federal regulators had allowed commercial banks to use off-balance-sheet entities to conduct most of their securitization functions. There is no doubt that this decision increased overall financial risk in the markets. It allowed for greater leverage, by allowing banks to conduct more securitization than if they had accounted for all the associated risks with *on*-balance-sheet charges, since doing the latter would have required higher equity capital.[381]

Many other federal policy decisions increased the financial risks that surfaced during the 2008 crisis. The following list provides a few examples of such policies, but it is far from inclusive.

- Banking regulators imposed the Basel capital requirements on all banks in 1988. These rules gave banks an incentive, through a preferential capital charge, to hold mortgage-backed securities instead of actual mortgages.[382]
- In 1991, the Federal Deposit Insurance Corporation Improvement Act allowed the Federal Reserve to make emergency loans to investment banks. The stated goal of the 1991 act was to shrink the so-called federal safety net for financial firms; however, this change expanded it.[383]
- In 1998, regulators changed the Basel capital rules with the market risk amendment, a change that, among other things, lowered the capital charge on mortgage-backed securities issued by the government-sponsored enterprises (GSEs) Fannie Mae and Freddie Mac, further incentivizing holding MBS (as opposed to actual mortgages).[384]
- Regulators amended banks' capital rules again in 2001, this time giving many private-label MBS the same low-risk weight as those GSE-issued MBS and extending preferential capital treatment to various other types of asset-backed securities. The rule is known as the recourse rule.[385]
- The 2005 Bankruptcy Abuse Prevention and Consumer Protection Act expanded several key safe harbors in bankruptcy law. As a result, firms using derivatives known as swaps, as well as repurchase agreements (repos), had preferred creditor status in any bankruptcy filing. At the very least, this change removed one reason for firms to fear using "too many" swaps or repos.[386]

The Big Short leaves the impression that greedy Wall Street financiers were out of control, unrelenting in their search of profits while wholly isolated from government rules. But government policy—which received a pass in *The Big Short*—undoubtedly deserves a share of the blame.

What's more perplexing, though, is that the 2008 financial crisis has been blamed on *deregulation*.

THE MYTH THAT NEEDS TO DIE:
FINANCIAL MARKET DEREGULATION

In his widely cited 1985 article *The Casino Society*, Anthony Bianco blames deregulation during the 1970s for hastening "the trader's rise to preeminence."[387] Popular historical accounts of the 1980s savings and loan crisis commonly blame "the free-market philosophy of the Reagan administration" and feature statements claiming that "Congress deregulated the banking industry."[388] And such critiques aren't just from the left side of the political spectrum. In 2023, the self-identified conservative activist group American Compass blamed the "increasingly complex and deregulated financial sector" for, among other things, "pulling capital out of the real economy . . . for purposes of financial engineering and speculation that generates enormous profits for the practitioners but nothing of value for the economy."[389] It should be no surprise, then, that scholars commonly attribute the 2008 crisis to a "deregulatory process" that began in the 1980s.[390]

This notion of deregulation in financial markets has taken hold among federal policymakers too. In 2008, for example, House Speaker Nancy Pelosi stated, "The [George W.] Bush Administration's eight long years of failed deregulation policies have resulted in our nation's largest bailout ever, leaving the American taxpayers on the hook potentially for billions of dollars."[391] Approximately one month later, in a presidential debate, Barack Obama asserted, "The biggest problem in this whole process was the deregulation of the financial system."[392] In 2009, Sen. Elizabeth Warren (D–MA) gave the following explanation for the cause of the 2008 crisis:

> It gets to be the early 1980s . . . and what do we do? Instead of saying "new products, we need to change regulations to adapt," we take a different path . . . we say "let's deregulate." . . . We begin to break down the old regulations, we say "who needs regulations, they're so poky, so old," so we go with this idea of let's get rid of regulation and what happens . . . and where do we end up? In the biggest crisis since the Great Depression.[393]

In fact, the idea that financial markets were deregulated before the 2008 financial crisis has essentially become conventional wisdom.

David Super, a professor of law and economics at Georgetown University, recently argued that deregulation is central to the agenda of both Republicans and "New Democrats" like President Bill Clinton. Super blamed both political parties for deregulating financial markets before the 2008 crisis, as well as for "relaxing Dodd-Frank standards" during the Trump administration.[394]

But if deregulation is taken to mean either the reduction or absence of regulation, it is easy to demonstrate that no major deregulation in US financial markets occurred during the past few decades or, for that matter, during the past century.

It is true that many changes to federal rules and regulations took place before the 2008 financial crisis. It is also true that some of the politicians responsible for those changes referred to their new policies as deregulatory. In fact, it is even true that some of those new policies allowed certain financial institutions to engage in activities previously forbidden to them. However, those *activities* were regulated before and after the new policies were implemented.

Yet it is definitively not the case that those new policies resulted in anything resembling deregulated financial markets. In many cases, financial institutions ended up with even more rules and regulation.

REGULATION INCREASED BEFORE 2008

The role of supposedly deregulated financial markets was central to the political narrative that explained the 2008 financial crisis and drove support for the 2010 Dodd-Frank Act. Nonetheless, although regulation can be measured in many ways, various metrics show that financial markets were not deregulated leading up to the 2008 financial crisis.

For instance, in rulemaking—the promulgation of specific rules by regulatory agencies—regulatory burdens climbed from 1999 through the 2008 crisis. In sheer volume, financial regulators issued 7,100 pages of regulations, containing more than 800 rules.[395] Moreover, financial regulations imposed a net cost on the economy for the eight years of the George W. Bush administration. In other words, even if some federal financial regulations during those eight years reduced regulatory burdens, the overall impact of the rules *increased* the cost of financial regulation. Data provided by the agencies themselves show that the major regulatory changes—defined as those with an economic effect of $100 million or more—cost the economy more than $2 billion (in constant 2010 dollars) from 2001 to 2008.[396]

Separately, the total budget of regulatory agencies increased. Excluding the Securities and Exchange Commission (SEC), the total budget of federal financial regulators increased by $300 million (15 percent) between 2000 and 2008, to almost $2.3 billion.[397] During the same period, the SEC's budget increased from $357 million to $629 million.[398] Total staffing at these agencies basically remained steady during this period, at nearly 16,000 employees.[399] At the SEC, however, the number of full-time-equivalent employees rose by 26 percent, to 3,568 in 2008.[400] Additionally, the Sarbanes-Oxley Act of 2002 created the Public Company Accounting Oversight Board, a nonprofit corporation that oversees the audits of public companies and SEC-registered brokers and dealers, the staff of which is not included in these totals. Thus, federal financial regulators' budgets increased, and, at best, their overall staff levels were not cut.[401]

These statistics for the George W. Bush administration are broadly consistent with longer-term trends. That is, long-term trends in both budget outlays and staffing suggest that regulation has been increasing steadily for decades. For example, federal outlays for banking and financial regulation increased from $190 million in 1960 to $1.9 billion in 2000, while staff rose from approximately 2,500 employees to more than 13,000.[402] Not surprisingly, many who claim that deregulated financial markets caused the crisis simply ignore these types of metrics and, instead, point to specific policy changes. In virtually all cases, though, these changes have been mischaracterized as deregulatory.

FEDERAL POLICYMAKERS DID NOT DEREGULATE

Broadly speaking—and in many specific instances—the regulatory changes that occurred in the decades before the 2008 financial crisis gave regulators *more* authority to tell financial firms what they can do and how they can do it. Some of these changes expanded the types of regulated activities in which certain firms could engage; however, only a gross misreading of the regulatory framework could consider these changes deregulatory. In virtually all instances, federal regulators were the official overseers of financial firms' activities both before and after the regulatory changes.

The following list provides a detailed summary of the most frequently cited policy changes that, supposedly, deregulated financial markets before the 2008 crisis.[403]

THE 1999 GRAMM-LEACH-BLILEY ACT (GLBA)

One of the most often-repeated claims is that the GLBA caused excessive risk taking because it repealed the Glass-Steagall Act, the 1933 law that separated commercial and investment banking.[404]

The first myth is that Glass-Steagall created an absolute separation between commercial and investment banking activities, but in fact, the act included myriad exceptions, so the separation between commercial and investment banking was never absolute. But more importantly, the GLBA, in amending the Glass-Steagall Act, did not deregulate financial market activities.[405]

The GLBA repealed two of the four sections of Glass-Steagall that implemented the so-called separation of commercial and investment banking. Sections 16 and 21 *generally* prohibited banks from underwriting or dealing in securities, and investment banking firms from accepting demand deposits, respectively.[406] Sections 20 and 32, on the other hand, *generally* prohibited commercial banks from affiliating with investment banks. Specifically, the GLBA repealed Sections 20 and 32 of the 1933 act, and left Sections 16 and 21 intact.[407] As a result of the GLBA, banks could legally affiliate with a company engaged in securities underwriting or dealing, but these different entity types could not engage in unregulated commercial or investment banking.

The GLBA also amended the Bank Holding Company Act of 1956, which gave the Federal Reserve the responsibility of regulating all bank holding companies, by allowing them to engage in a broader range of financial activities than previously.[408] The GLBA defined many activities as being financial in nature and prohibited certain nonfinancial activities. Section 103 of the GLBA, for example, specified various activities *and* vested the Fed and Treasury with discretionary authority to determine whether an activity was financial in nature.

The GLBA required bank holding companies to register with the Federal Reserve if they wanted to legally engage in these activities. Additionally, a bank holding company could only be approved to operate after (among other requirements) the Fed certified that both the holding company and all its subsidiary depository institutions were well managed and well capitalized and in compliance with the Community Reinvestment Act.[409]

The GLBA also contained five unrelated titles that, in many instances, increased financial regulations. Title IV of the GLBA prohibited the creation of new thrift holding companies as well as the sale of existing thrift holding companies to any nonfinancial firm. Title V instituted new privacy and disclosure regulations, including new civil penalties.[410] This title also amended the capital rules for banks in the Federal Home Loan Bank (FHLB) System. For instance, Title V made the FHLB's capital structure more permanent by requiring members to invest their capital for five years, and subjected FHLBs to new leverage and risk-based capital requirements.[411] Title VII implemented many provisions, including new Community Reinvestment Act requirements for banks and the requirement for ATM operators to post fee notices both on the machine and on the screen.

THE 1980 DEPOSITORY INSTITUTIONS DEREGULATION AND MONETARY CONTROL ACT (DMCA)

The DMCA is often described as a deregulatory bill mainly because it phased out interest-rate ceilings on savings and time deposits at commercial banks and thrifts. Those price controls had been in place since the 1930s as part of Congress's efforts to prevent large banks from engaging in speculative activity, to limit competition for deposits, and to encourage rural banks to lend more within their communities.[412] For three decades, the ceiling had little impact because it was kept above short-term market rates, but it never worked as designed.

In the 1960s, as market rates began to increase, policy failure started to become more obvious. Rather than get rid of the ceiling,

Congress responded by expanding the ceiling to savings and thrift institutions.[413] Congress tried to use these price controls to stop interest rates
on capital markets from rising and to expand access to mortgage credit,
but the price controls did not achieve those objectives. Worse, wealthier
savers—who typically have large deposit balances—started moving money
out of banks.[414] During the 1970s, interest rates rose even more steeply,
and the rate ceilings led to a disastrous disintermediation of the banking
sector—so many people moved their money out of banks and into capital
markets that it left the entire banking system depleted of capital and of the
funds needed to pay customers and make additional loans.[415] Thus, critics
often refer to the removal of these price controls as part of a broad deregulatory effort; however, that view obscures a major policy failure that
essentially forced Congress to reverse course with price controls.

Regardless, the DMCA included many other provisions that
increased regulations. For instance, the DMCA made *all* depository
institutions subject to the Fed's deposit reserve requirements. Before this
change, only Federal Reserve member institutions were subject to the
Fed's reserve regulations. The DMCA required a given bank or thrift
to hold its reserves in an account at its Federal Reserve District Bank,
subject to the Fed's rules, regardless of whether it chose to be a member
of the Federal Reserve System.[416]

Although the question of membership is largely ignored now, the
Fed was losing member banks for *more than two decades* leading up to the
passage of the DMCA—between 1970 and 1978, roughly 300 banks left
the Fed system, and the ratio of members' deposits to total bank deposits
fell from more than 80 percent to 72 percent.[417] This one law, though,
expanded the Fed's control from 5,600 depository institutions to almost
40,000, with more than twice the amount of total assets.[418]

At best, the DMCA's overall effect could be viewed as ambiguous,
but certainly not deregulatory.[419]

THE 1982 GARN–ST. GERMAIN DEPOSITORY INSTITUTIONS ACT

The Garn–St. Germain Act is frequently cited as deregulatory because it
allowed certain thrifts to make commercial loans, a practice from which
they were previously restricted. Viewed in the proper context, however,

the act was a rescue bill for the thrift industry and an acceleration of the 1980 DMCA. In other words, to allow savings and loan institutions to earn higher profits in the hope of staving off industry-wide failures, Congress expanded thrifts' regulated activities. Ultimately, the gambit failed, and regulators allowed insolvent S&Ls to remain open longer than they otherwise would have.[420]

Titles I and II of the act enhanced the powers of the FDIC and FSLIC (Federal Savings and Loan Insurance Corporation) to provide aid to failing and failed institutions.[421] Title III—the main source of the bill's deregulatory characterization—authorized federally chartered S&Ls and savings banks (thrifts) to make commercial loans. It permitted, for the first time, the S&Ls to offer demand deposits to their loan customers. But the act did not allow thrifts to make loans or offer demand deposits in a *deregulated* manner.[422] Indeed, S&Ls were required to conduct these activities subject to the rules and regulations of the Federal Home Loan Bank Board.

Title III also created the money market deposit account (MMDA), a concession designed to allow banks to better compete with nonbank money market mutual funds. Although MMDAs had no interest-rate ceilings, they became subject to rules and regulations, including minimum account balances and limits on the type and number of transfers (six per month, of which no more than three could be by check).

Title IV of the law has also been referred to as deregulatory because it supposedly "relaxed" certain limitations on the size of loans that national banks could make to any one borrower.[423] It makes little sense to call this change deregulatory, though, because Title IV merely raised the *maximum allowed* percentage from 10 percent to 15 percent of an institution's capital and surplus. After the act was passed, *all* national depository institutions' loans still had to comply with the rules and regulations promulgated by their primary regulator.

THE 1994 RIEGLE-NEAL INTERSTATE BANKING AND BRANCHING EFFICIENCY ACT (IBBEA)

The IBBEA is often cited as deregulatory because it removed restrictions on interstate branching by banks. It did not, however, allow these newly branched banks to function in an unregulated environment. In other words, the same banking activities were regulated by the same banking regulators both before and after the IBBEA was passed.

Before the Civil War, bank regulation was largely a state matter, and few states allowed interstate banking. However, limited interstate travel and communication opportunities then made interstate banking impractical.[424] It also became clearer at the time that having a system dominated by small banks tied to their local economies—the unit banking system— was not sound. In a sense, both practical experience and technological changes pushed Congress to enact the IBBEA.

The IBBEA also gave new regulatory authority to the Fed for some of the key branching activities that it newly allowed, such as a bank holding company's acquiring a bank outside its home state.[425] Separately, activities such as interstate bank mergers and opening of new branches had to be approved by the appropriate federal regulator (either the comptroller of the currency, the Fed, or the FDIC).[426] The IBBEA provided regulators some discretion in these new activities and placed several statutory restrictions on interstate banking, including nationwide and state concentration limits on total deposits at one institution.[427]

Regardless, the IBBEA merely revamped regulation; it did not deregulate banking activity.

THE 2000 COMMODITY FUTURES MODERNIZATION ACT (CFMA)

The CFMA is frequently cited as deregulatory because the bill prevented the CFTC from regulating over-the-counter (OTC) derivatives, such as swaps. It is true that, under the CFMA, the CFTC did not regulate many OTC derivatives, but it makes little sense to call the law deregulatory because the CFTC did not regulate these derivatives *before* the passage of the CFMA. Furthermore, one of the main purposes of the CFMA was to clarify which regulator, the CFTC or the SEC, would regulate *single-stock futures contracts*. These financial products have features of both securities and commodities, items that fall under the separate jurisdictions of the SEC and the CFTC.[428]

Before the passage of the CFMA, the main legal uncertainty surrounding swaps was whether they could be construed as futures under the Commodity Exchange Act. Many feared that such a classification would void contracts if they were traded in the OTC market (off-exchange), as they had been for years.[429] Regardless, even the OTC swaps in question were regulated. In fact, the bulk of the swaps market—even the infamous credit default swaps associated with the 2008 financial crisis—were regulated by *banking* regulators because banks were their main users.[430]

Historically, interest-rate and foreign exchange swaps used by large banks had accounted for more than 80 percent of the OTC derivatives market.[431] In 2000, just as now, federal banking regulators constantly monitored banks' financial condition, including the banks' swaps exposure.[432] In fact, the very first iteration of the Basel capital requirements, implemented in the late 1980s, required banks to account for their swaps when calculating regulatory capital ratios. Banks had to hold capital against the *credit-risk equivalent* to the swaps, essentially treating them the same as other loans in their risk-adjusted assets.[433]

None of these swap transactions took place outside bank regulators' purview, and the public record attests to this fact. For instance, a 1993 Boston Federal Reserve paper noted, "Bank regulators have recognized the credit risk of swaps and instituted capital requirements for them and for other off-balance-sheet activities, as part of the new risk-based capital requirements for banks."[434] Similarly, a 1996 OCC guidance bulletin stated:

> Bank management must ensure that credit derivatives are incorporated into their risk-based capital (RBC) computation. Over the near-term, the RBC treatment of a credit derivative will be determined on a case-by-case basis through a review of the specific characteristics of the transaction. For example, banks should note that some forms of credit derivatives are functionally equivalent to standby letters of credit or similar types of financial enhancements. However, other forms might be treated like interest rate, equity, or other commodity derivatives, which have a different RBC requirement.[435]

After the CFMA was enacted, the regulatory situation remained largely the same. For instance, a 2006 OCC report stated:

> As a result, derivatives activity is appropriately concentrated in those few institutions that have made the resource commitment to operate the business in a safe and sound manner. Further, the OCC has

examiners on site in these large banks to evaluate the credit, market, operational, reputation and compliance risks in the derivatives portfolio on an ongoing basis.[436]

Even the controversial credit default swaps used by the failed insurance company American International Group—better known as AIG—took place under the watchful eye of the Office of Thrift Supervision, a federal banking regulator whose responsibilities Dodd–Frank transferred to the OCC, the Fed, and the FDIC.[437] The notion that these swap transactions took place in some shadowy room where regulators had no clue what was going on is false. Nonetheless, Title VII of Dodd–Frank gave the CFTC and the SEC authority to regulate the OTC swaps markets.[438]

THE 2004 AMENDMENT TO THE SEC'S NET CAPITAL RULE

Sections 8(b) and 15(c)(3) of the 1934 Securities Exchange Act introduced a net capital rule for broker-dealers that dictates the type and amount of liquid assets that broker-dealers must maintain. The rule was amended several times after 1934, including a major adjustment in 1975 after a series of firm failures in the late 1960s and early 1970s. It was amended again in 2004.[439] The 2004 rule change has been lumped in with the supposedly deregulatory policies that contributed to the 2008 crisis, and also blamed for allowing broker-dealers to raise their leverage—debt— to dangerously high levels. Nonetheless, data show that major investment banks were *more* highly leveraged in 1998 than in 2006.[440]

Regardless of how the rule change affected these firms' leverage, it is, once again, highly misleading to characterize this amendment as deregulatory. The main component of the 2004 rule change allowed for an alternative method for computing deductions under the broker-dealer net capital rule.[441] It is true that the rule allowed firms to use mathematical models to calculate their net capital requirements, but these firms were still subject to a minimum capital rule. Furthermore, companies electing to use the alternative approach were also subjected to "enhanced net capital, early warning, recordkeeping, reporting, and certain other requirements."[442] Finally, all firms using the alternative method were required to implement and document an internal risk management system. The overall intent of the 2004 rule change was to allow the SEC to regulate holding companies on a consolidated basis, much like the Fed does with bank holding companies.[443] Regardless, the change only applied to holding companies that did not already have a principal regulator, and it did not remove leverage restrictions.[444]

As this discussion demonstrates, the most frequently cited "deregulatory" policy changes that supposedly contributed to the 2008 crisis did not deregulate financial markets. Some critics—perhaps recognizing the level of regulation in place before 2008—have made more subtle arguments about the shortcomings of the regulatory framework.

THE "BETTER" REGULATION MYTH
AND THE 2008 CRISIS

The conventional view points to deregulation as a main cause of the 2008 crisis; however, a related view holds that regulators were simply engaged in the wrong *type* of regulation. Specifically, policymakers argued that, in the future, regulators could reduce the chances of a crisis by broadening their focus to *system-wide*—that is, systemic—risk, rather than concentrating on individual firm risk.[445] In fact, just before the 2008 bankruptcy of Lehman Brothers, the Fed chair Ben Bernanke remarked at the Fed's famous Jackson Hole conference:

> Going forward, a critical question for regulators and supervisors is what their appropriate "field of vision" should be. Under our current system of safety-and-soundness regulation, supervisors often focus on the financial conditions of individual institutions in isolation. An alternative approach, which has been called systemwide or macroprudential oversight, would broaden the mandate of regulators and supervisors to encompass consideration of potential systemic risks and weaknesses as well.[446]

At best, the claim that this policy shift would represent a new, or alternative, focus is highly misleading. Although it is true that the Basel III capital rules, implemented in the United States in 2013, employ some systemic risk (macroprudential) regulations that were not previously used in the United States, the concept of regulators' focusing on systemic risk is not new—and it wasn't new in 2008. One of the main justifications for creating the Fed—to say nothing of the extensive federal regulatory framework that has been constructed over the past century—was to prevent problems in the financial sector from spilling over to the broader economy.

Unsurprisingly, the Fed, Congress, and the US Treasury have openly discussed their roles in stemming economy-wide systemic risk and financial stability for decades. For instance, regulators' focus on systemic risk was clear during the 1984 congressional hearings in the wake of the Continental Illinois National Bank bailout. At those hearings, the comptroller of the currency Todd Conover testified that the bank supervisor's role was to maintain *systemic soundness*:

> Our [the OCC's] supervision of banks of all sizes has been enhanced by the establishment of an Industry Review Program. This program includes a computerized information system to collect data on industry concentrations in individual bank portfolios and *the banking system as a whole.*[447]
>
> . . . In addition to the more frequent examinations we have undertaken, the examiners will also monitor trends and developments in the banks between examinations. This new approach results in near-constant supervision of each of our large banks. We are now better able to identify and devote attention to items of supervisory concern in individual large banks and significant practices emerging in *the large bank population as a whole.*[448]

The OCC was not the only federal regulator concerned with systemic risk before the 2008 crisis.[449] For instance, John LaWare, a Federal Reserve Board governor, testified regarding systemic-risk concerns before the House Subcommittee on Economic Stabilization in 1991, shortly after the Basel I Accord was completed. He told Congress, "One of the fundamental purposes of our banking safety net is to prevent systemic risk from becoming an observable reality."[450] He then referenced Federal Reserve Chair Alan Greenspan's House testimony from the prior week regarding the Board of Governors' views on reducing systemic risk, and stated, "By increasing the safety and soundness of our banking system, these reforms would lessen the likelihood of a major systemic threat and a need to invoke too–big–to–fail."[451]

In 1996, federal regulators adopted an even more explicit systemic risk acknowledgment. Specifically, the Fed started to account for system-wide risk by altering its rating system for financial institutions. After the change, the system was known as the CAMELS rating. Before the change, the system was known as the "CAMEL" rating—the 1996 change added the S, which stood for *sensitivity to market risk*.[452]

In reality, this supposedly newfound concern over systemic risk reflects the desire to implement "better" capital requirements to prevent the next crisis. In practice, this approach amounts to little more than placing higher capital requirements on specific firms for undertaking financial activities that regulators perceive to be higher risk. Put differently, the idea amounts to tailoring capital requirements for individual firms to increase system-wide financial stability, just as regulators have done for decades. (Federal banking regulators' latest proposed revision to banks' capital rules, announced in September 2023, confirms this conclusion.[453])

Tailoring capital requirements to increase system-wide financial stability may sound like a plausible approach; however, history suggests that Americans should not depend on better capital requirements to prevent future crises.

The 1983 International Lending Supervision Act, for example, represented a major effort toward reducing financial instability with higher and more appropriately tailored capital requirements. The law gave federal regulators the explicit authority to regulate banks' capital adequacy, and to define what constitutes adequate capital levels.[454] Soon after the act was passed, Comptroller of the Currency Todd Conover testified to Congress, "In the first quarter of 1984 the average ratio of primary capital to total assets stood at 5.67 percent . . . almost 16 percent higher than the average level at those banks two years ago."[455] In 1988, federal regulators adopted the first iteration of the Basel rules, which were designed to better match capital requirements with the risk level of financial assets. Regulators were in the process of implementing the supposedly improved Basel II rules, which the 2008 financial crisis exposed as flawed.[456] Regulators then stopped that process and went to work on developing Basel III instead.

Whether the new rules perform better is an open question, but all three iterations of the Basel rules rely on similar types of subjective risk assessments. In fact, the original Basel rules were crafted based partly on the "risk bucket" approach developed by the Federal Reserve in the 1950s, so the Basel risk-weight approach itself is not entirely new.[457] Regardless, the flawed nature of this approach was exposed in 2001, when the Fed, jointly with the FDIC and OCC, amended risk-based capital rules so that banks could hold less capital for highly rated privately issued mortgage-backed securities.

After the 2001 rule change, certain AA- and AAA-rated asset-backed securities were given the same low-risk weight (20 percent) as Fannie- and Freddie-issued mortgage-backed securities because regulators thought the former were low risk.[458] Regardless of whether this rule change contributed to the 2008 crisis, it is undeniable that US commercial banks exceeded their minimum capital requirements by two to three percentage points for six years leading up to the 2008 crisis.[459] It is exceedingly difficult, therefore, to argue that the risk-weighted capital approach has worked as designed. Regulators had the wrong risk weights on the assets at the center of the 2008 crisis, and the fact that banks exceeded their capital requirements did not prevent a crisis and long-term economic slowdown.

CONCLUSION

The conventional narrative is that deregulated financial markets have caused all kinds of problems in the past few decades, most notably the 2008 financial crisis. According to this story, the events leading up to the crisis took place in the shadows, outside the view of financial regulators. The supposed problem was Wall Street's unabated pursuit of profit, with no regard for anything or anyone else, through risky and impenetrable securities that only the traders understood. And the deregulatory administrations of Ronald Reagan and George W. Bush left regulators powerless to stop them. This deregulation and capitalists-gone-rogue story quickly became the conventional explanation of the 2008 financial crisis, and it drove popular support for the 2010 Dodd–Frank Act.

As this chapter has demonstrated, though, the conventional explanation of the 2008 financial crisis is wrong. Simply put, financial market deregulation did not cause the 2008 financial crisis because financial markets were not deregulated. No appreciable reduction has occurred in either the scope or the volume of regulation in US financial markets during the past 100-plus years. Moreover, even the regulatory changes that occurred during the Reagan and George W. Bush administrations helped cement an ever-expanding financial regulatory framework. Some of these changes did allow financial firms to engage in activities that were previously prohibited, but they were only permitted to do so under the watchful eye of regulators.

Nothing close to a deregulated financial market exists in the United States, and it certainly did not exist before the 2008 crisis. Virtually all financial firms' activities—including those that contributed to the 2008 crisis—occur in a highly regulated environment.

In short, the regulatory changes that took place in the decades before the 2008 financial crisis gave regulators *more* authority to tell financial firms what they can do and how they can do it.

Moreover, Congress has increasingly moved the regulatory framework in this direction since at least the 1930s, increasingly micromanaging financial firms' activities. The next chapter discusses the justification for such a regulatory approach. It then discusses an alternative approach.

Chapter 7
A Better Approach
to Financial Regulation

Many people view the relationship between regulators and business as adversarial, a view that is not entirely unfounded. Some might be surprised, though, to learn that financial firms—especially incumbent ones—rarely support deregulation and free markets. For instance, in 2013, JPMorganChase CEO Jamie Dimon acknowledged that the new regulations mandated by the Dodd-Frank Act could shrink his bank's profit margins. Yet he wasn't overly concerned because he thought the higher costs would eventually increase JPMorganChase's market share. Smaller firms, Dimon reasoned, would have the most trouble dealing with the higher regulatory costs, so Dodd-Frank's requirements would ultimately put a "bigger moat" around his bank, one that would help keep out smaller competitors.[460]

In fact, this favorable view is not unique to the biggest financiers of Wall Street. Believe it or not, the Independent Community Bankers of America (ICBA) helped get the Dodd-Frank bill through Congress. When the bill was still being put together, the ICBA's president Cam Fine made a deal with Rep. Barney Frank (D-MA). Fine assured Frank that the ICBA would support—or, at least, not oppose—the bill provided that the new consumer protection agency—what eventually became the Consumer Financial Protection Bureau—would have supervisory powers *only* for banks with assets greater than $10 billion, thus exempting most of the ICBA's small banks from additional federal supervision. Fine also won a change to the Federal Deposit Insurance Corporation (FDIC) deposit coverage assessment that saved small banks more than $1 billion per year. Both of these concessions came at the expense of larger banks.[461]

Other financial trade associations and professionals regularly exhibit a kind of "go along to get along" approach with Congress and federal agencies. For example, in 2011, the CEO of the Securities Industry and Financial Markets Association (SIFMA), Tim Ryan, expressed his members' acceptance of Dodd-Frank. He said: "Today, the industry's view as expressed by SIFMA is Dodd-Frank is the law. We are all about providing substantive input so that the government produces final regulations that make sense."[462] At some level, this approach makes sense, because regulators have enormous discretionary authority over financial firms and financial firms have countless repeat interactions with their regulator. It's not hard to see that it often doesn't pay to be adversarial. Though perhaps an extreme illustration, when the Dodd-Frank rules were being developed, a group of more than 40 securities defense lawyers even lobbied on behalf of the regulator, asking Congress to increase the Securities and Exchange Commission (SEC) budget so that investors would not view the SEC as an inadequate regulator.[463]

These examples may seem surprising, but the financiers of Wall Street—*and* Main Street—generally do not lobby for deregulation. These firms do not want a free market. They, like many other types of businesses, accept that they will be heavily regulated. As a result, they spend much of their time fighting—often successfully—for rules that benefit their bottom line, often at the expense of their competition and, ultimately, consumers. Nonetheless, the perception of Wall Street as a bastion of support for free markets persists, as do many other myths surrounding financial regulation.

To begin with, the notion that the regulatory framework has been created by agnostic or benevolent overseers is simply incorrect. Rather, the framework is the result of a series of political deals. Previous chapters chronicled how these deals have shaped the regulatory framework throughout American history. In the words of scholars Charles Calomiris and Stephen Haber, the regulatory framework is the "product of political deals that determine which laws are passed and which groups of people have licenses to contract with whom, for what, and on what terms."[464]

At the very least, this situation is cause for concern, because political deals are regularly made by politicians who skillfully tell people what they want them to hear rather than how policymaking really works. The situation is more dire, though, for at least two reasons.

First, financial regulation, at its core, is about giving a small group of people the power to determine what everybody else can do with their money. The people with the most at stake—not the typical American worker—have the most say in how that process unfolds, often resulting in less competition in the financial sector and less freedom for people to use their money as they desire. Over time, regulation increases in volume and complexity, blocking the primary benefits that free markets provide, including widespread increases in productivity and living standards.

Second, poorly thought-out financial regulations have a history of *creating* financial turmoil.

These facts are often underappreciated, though, because policymakers justify regulation as necessary for ensuring financial stability, and few people understand the details of the regulatory framework or how it is created. Indeed, as that framework grows, it makes little sense for the typical American to study its details. (In economics parlance, this phenomenon is known as "rational ignorance." Why, for example, would any normal person outside the banking industry study a 300-page regulation on one small slice of federal bank capital requirements?) As a result, increasing regulation and federal backing have been the norm for decades in financial markets.[465]

Support for this approach is based on the idea that banking and finance are inherently unstable businesses, and that a more highly regulated system, with increased government backing, can prevent or mitigate financial crises and any associated economic fallout.[466] Additionally, many argue that bank failures pose a special threat because they can easily spill over to the rest of the economy. Either way, extensive government regulation is, supposedly, necessary to maintain financial stability.[467]

This notion that the government must protect people from freely operating financial markets has guided US bank regulation for most of the country's history, and it has increasingly encroached on US capital market regulation since the 1930s. Advocates of more regulation and federal support for financial institutions should have a difficult hurdle to overcome, because—as decades of experience show—as regulators have taken on a more active role in managing financial firms' risk taking, financial crises have not subsided in tandem. It is now indisputable that *if* this kind of framework can maintain financial stability, it has not done so yet.

Despite a history of failure, many also see extensive regulations as necessary to protect taxpayers from having to cover any shortfalls in the FDIC's Deposit Insurance Fund.[468] This argument assumes that federal deposit insurance is necessary to maintain financial stability. And, in fact, many believe that *both* federal support and extensive regulation for financial markets are necessary to maintain stability. Many advocates of this policy combination openly call for the full government provisioning of money and the federal backing of essentially all short-term credit markets.

For example, legal scholars Morgan Ricks and Lev Menand want regulators to "clarify banks' place in U.S. society and their relation to the government," such that all money becomes "a governmental product." They actively hail a "new monetary era" with central bank digital currencies, a digital version of the dollar that ties citizens directly to the government.[469] Saule Omarova, whom President Biden nominated for comptroller of the currency in 2021, has called for "the complete migration of demand deposit accounts [at commercial banks] to the Fed's balance sheet."[470] Omarova acknowledges that the "compositional over-haul of the Fed's balance sheet would fundamentally alter the operations and systemic footprints of private banks, funds, derivatives dealers, and other financial institutions and markets."[471] Yet she believes that such reforms would "make the financial system more inclusive, efficient, and stable."[472]

This kind of "overhaul" would create a financial market profoundly different from the one that currently exists in America. Although many aspects of US financial markets consist of a public–private arrangement, this kind of change would all but eliminate the private portion. Such a new arrangement would give a select few untold economic and political power over everyone else. Yet time and again, regulators have already demonstrated an inability to craft rules and regulations that maintain financial stability. And there is little to suggest that those at the regulatory agencies will do a better job managing financial risk than those participating in financial markets with their own money at stake.

Not all advocates of stricter financial regulation and federal backing want the kind of public system envisioned by critics such as Ricks, Menand, and Omarova; however, the long-term trend has pushed in that direction. Indeed, once systemic risk became a main justification for regulation and government backing, such a shift became all but inevitable. When two regional banks failed in 2023, for instance, the federal government evoked a "systemic risk exception" that allowed the FDIC to cover even the *uninsured* deposits (amounts larger than the $250,000 coverage limit) at those banks, all in the name of maintaining financial stability.[473] Although government officials making these kinds of decisions likely have the best of intentions, the long-run effect of more regulation and government support has been negative for many Americans.

The existing system protects incumbent firms from new competition, thus working against the very market forces that spur innovation, reduce prices, and prevent excessive risk taking. Entrepreneurs and workers have suffered from fewer economic opportunities, and consumers have suffered from fewer choices, higher prices, and less awareness of financial risks. Each time the system crashes, as it has done on multiple occasions, human beings naturally tend to blame excesses in the private sector. Spurred on by political leaders, it becomes easy to acquiesce to more government supervision over financial matters in the name of stabilizing the economy. Ultimately, this process has been a perverse self-reinforcing cycle, one that fails to make the economy any safer, as it chips away at economic freedom and the prosperity such freedom fosters.

Policymakers could undertake a long list of reforms to move the system in the other direction, closer to a free market with less government backing and regulation. And they could do so without fear of undue instability—the existing framework only provides a false sense of security. Naturally, Americans should not expect a move toward a free market, or even a pure free market, to produce utopian-like outcomes, devoid of bankruptcies and financial instability. But the existing system—which is not a free market by any means—is far from devoid of bankruptcies or instability and is far closer to a government-directed system than is warranted.

PRIVATE MARKETS AND SIMPLE RULES OUTPERFORM THE CURRENT US REGULATORY FRAMEWORK

Though most members of Congress would balk at federally insuring the profits and strictly regulating the daily operations of firms such as Home Depot, Walmart, and Apple, most members are at least complicit in setting up such rules in the financial sector. These regulations are justified on the notion that financial firms are different. The truth, though, is that financial firms are no more special, or dangerous, than nonfinancial companies. Each group of companies needs the other, and each would suffer in isolation. The evidence suggests that without federal deposit insurance, even *banks* are not particularly special. As Loyola University Chicago economist George Kaufman argued, "There is no evidence to support the widely held belief that, even in the absence of deposit insurance, bank contagion is a holocaust that can bring down solvent banks, the financial system, and even the entire macroeconomy in domino fashion."[474] A much better approach, as in other sectors of the economy, would be to base financial regulation on protecting individuals and firms from fraud and violations of contractual rights, not prescriptive merit-based regulation or micromanagement of firms' activities.

This approach would be quite different from the current US financial regulatory framework, which is highly flawed. Its exceedingly prescriptive federal rules provide a false sense of security because the government confers an aura of safety on all firms that play by the rules. This is a problem for three major reasons: (a) people take on more risk than they would in the absence of such rules, (b) human beings have lower incentives to monitor financial risks than they would otherwise, and (c) compared with other actors in the market, regulators do not have superior knowledge of future risks.[475] For these reasons, the existing system has already proved incapable of maintaining financial stability, so policymakers should reverse course.

More broadly, the view that private markets are inherently unstable and prone to turmoil, thus requiring government support, is at best incomplete, and at worst misguided.[476] It is incomplete because it ignores the institutional arrangements that have been created in the absence of a free market. To varying degrees, these arrangements prevent people from taking advantage of their own opportunities by giving a small group of people power to determine what everyone else is allowed to do.

In their extreme form, such arrangements are akin to a feudal system, where hardly anyone outside a small group has any wealth. In the American system, which is nothing like a feudal system, the average citizen has lost a large degree of economic freedom and some amount of wealth but has not gained the stability that was promised in return.[477] Arguably, the current level of regulation and government support in the United States is most harmful to those with lower incomes and less wealth—they have given up the same economic freedoms but likely suffer more from the loss of opportunity, especially during times of economic turmoil. Regardless, Americans have continued losing more of their economic freedoms in matters of finance—they have less and less ability to do with their money as they please—without gaining the promised benefit of stability. All the while, regulators have continued to expand their already far-ranging jurisdiction and power, partly because Congress has given them so much discretionary authority.

Although regulators do need some discretion and flexibility to make basic enforcement decisions, the scope of federal regulators' discretionary authority is far from narrowly tailored. This situation is problematic precisely because it has fostered the growth of complex and evolving rules rather than simple and clear ones. For instance, US law now mandates federal financial regulators to guard against *threats* to financial stability, yet it fails to define threats *or* financial stability. This kind of ill-defined mandate could easily be used to justify wide-ranging government intervention in the financial sector without any additional congressional input.[478]

Climate change policy is perhaps the best recent example of where regulatory discretion and ill-defined financial stability mandates could result in extensive new government intervention in financial markets to further a political agenda. For example, in a 2020 journal article, Stanford law professor Graham Steele, who went on to serve in the Biden Treasury Department, discusses the legal authorities that regulators now have and argues, "In failing to fully appreciate the potential risks of climate change and their responsibility to mitigate them, regulators' current approach is reminiscent of the pre-[2008]crisis period."[479] Steele then argues that if regulators fail to implement "effective macroprudential climate policies," then they are "providing a nontransparent, indirect subsidy to climate change–causing industries."[480]

As Steele affirms, there are multiple legal avenues that US regulators could use to implement a climate change policy agenda. Regarding the 2010 Dodd-Frank Act, he explains that it "codifies the terms 'financial stability' and 'systemic risk' into law, but it offers no comprehensive definitions and delegates significant discretionary authority to regulatory agencies to determine the meaning of those terms and the measures to be taken to address them."[481] Steele then lists several sections of the *United States Code* that federal regulators could use to implement climate change policies, and offers multiple examples. The list includes actions that the Financial Stability Oversight Council and the Federal Reserve each could take. For instance, the Financial Stability Oversight Council could designate nonbank financial firms for special regulation by the Fed, and the Fed could "*limit fossil fuel investments* on the basis of their prospective risks to financial stability," and "force the largest, most systemic bank holding companies, insurers, and asset managers to divest of their climate change–causing assets."[482]

Whereas Steele focuses on using regulatory discretion to implement *climate change* policies through financial regulation, that same discretion could be used to implement practically any political agenda.[483] Indeed, during the Obama administration, federal banking regulators used their discretionary authority in Operation Choke Point—a multiagency initiative led by the Justice Department—to pressure banks to stop dealing with small-dollar lenders and other politically disfavored businesses. Many banks dropped those customers as a result. In this case, regulators relied on their discretionary authorities regarding "reputational risk" and "safety and soundness." They explicitly argued that dealing with such customers endangered both the banks' reputation and safety and soundness, a claim that banks are in no position to rebut.[484]

Separately, federal banking regulators have used discretionary authority to make banks wary of dealing with digital asset firms, which make up a small part of financial markets.[485] Whatever merits this authority may have, there is no doubt that these recent actions have kept banks isolated from competing with new digital payment companies, thus isolating them from the competitive forces that would otherwise push them to innovate and improve their products and services.

Enshrining these vague concepts into law was a mistake that should be corrected. Ambitious regulators can find threats to financial stability, reputational risk, or safety and soundness in virtually any scenario. This kind of ill-defined authority gives a relatively small number of people—who are largely unaccountable to voters—enormous power over how Americans conduct their lives. These concepts should be removed from the regulatory framework, and Congress should replace them with clear and simple rules that do not provide regulators with such far-ranging discretion. Reforms should be judged against the following 10 core principles regarding financial markets and regulation.[486]

CORE PRINCIPLES

1. Competitive financial markets are essential for creating widespread improvements in people's living standards.
2. The government should not interfere with the financial choices of market participants, including consumers, investors, and financial firms not insured by the government. Regulators should focus on protecting individuals and firms from fraud and violations of contractual rights.

3. Market discipline is a better regulator of financial risk than government regulation.

4. Financial firms should be permitted to fail, just as other firms do. The government should not "save" participants from failure because doing so impedes the ability of markets to direct resources to their highest and best use.

5. Speculation and risk taking are what make markets operate. Interference by regulators attempting to mitigate risks hinders the effective operation of markets.

6. The government should not make credit and capital allocation decisions.

7. The cost of financial firm failures should be borne by managers, equity holders, and creditors, not by taxpayers.

8. Simple rules—such as straightforward equity capital requirements—are preferable to complex rules that permit regulators to micromanage markets.

9. Public–private partnerships create financial instability because they create rent-seeking opportunities and misalign incentives.

10. Government backing for financial activities, such as classifying certain firms or activities as "systemically important," inevitably leads to government bailouts.

Admittedly, changes that adhere to these principles will be controversial, and perhaps none will be as divisive as the third principle, that market discipline is a better regulator of financial risk than government regulation. As this book has demonstrated, though, the evidence is on the side of private markets versus government-controlled financial markets. The massive regulatory framework has not eliminated financial turmoil, and the federal government has repeatedly forced taxpayers to cover losses for large financial firms and investors.

The theory behind this third principle is often obscure, but it hinges on the fact that rules would still exist without a massive government regulatory framework—markets set standards and enforce rules through cooperation and competition. Governments, on the other hand, set standards by centralizing legal rules and requirements. And while both markets and governments make mistakes, markets have more flexibility to analyze and adapt. Government rules are often sweeping and difficult to change.

As a result, market discipline suffers under the government-based approach. Where more market-based activities would normally provide improvements through cooperation and competition, they are unable to do so. Where the fear of unmitigated loss would normally place a check on financial risk, it no longer does so. All the while, the harmful rules that restrict these powerful market forces and increase financial risk become entrenched, damaging the structure of financial markets—they become more fragile and less productive than they would be if people were exposed to more market discipline.

CONCLUSION

Vague concepts like systemic risk and safety and soundness, combined with countless detailed rules and requirements for operating procedures, have created a regulatory framework at odds with limited government and free enterprise. Because the framework creates enormous entry costs for new financial firms, and because the largest firms and investors are protected in the name of stability, the framework is inherently anti-competitive. And because the framework is anti-competitive, it isolates incumbent firms from the very forces that provide the main benefits of a free enterprise system. Over time, the system has progressively narrowed the scope of what people can do with their money, such that an increasingly smaller number of people now control how most people can invest, when they can invest, and even who gets to invest. This framework has consistently been expanded in the name of protecting the system, but it has never worked as promised.

Instead, it has done the opposite. It has made the system more fragile, and it has made it more difficult for most people to invest and build wealth. A dramatic change is needed to increase the kind of financial diversity that makes a financial system more resilient, in a way that offers more people greater choice and opportunity. Critics claim that the average citizen could not possibly have the knowledge necessary to make good financial decisions under a less regulated financial market, but this condescending view ignores that the existing rules and regulations are too complex and voluminous for the average person to assess how they affect his or her own personal welfare.

The system should no longer be based on maintaining financial stability through government backing or regulation. It should no longer be based on the idea that financial firms are special compared with the rest of the economy. There is no objective economic justification for this kind of system, and the same arguments for heavily regulating and supporting financial firms could easily be applied to all nonfinancial firms. The number of people who would potentially lose their ability to earn a living if, for example, Walmart, Apple, or Ford closed, is no less an economic concern than if Citibank were to go bankrupt. The failure of any of these companies would endanger the well-being of millions of people who depend on them for a living. A system based on using government regulation and support to ensure widespread economic stability for all industries is not a free enterprise system. Most people living in such a system have very little economic opportunity and very limited choice in how they can live their lives.

In one sense, it is good that many members of Congress are comfortable limiting extensive government regulation and control to financial markets, rather than to *all* businesses. Ultimately, though, that approach is no better because it will increasingly encroach on citizens' freedom regarding financial decisions and, eventually, all other economic decisions. The longer the current trajectory is maintained, the further from a free enterprise system the US economy will drift, endangering Americans' widespread prosperity.

The sooner the current trajectory is reversed, the more weight that policy can give to people's ability to manage their own safety and make their own choices. Although many policymakers fear such an approach, the current system gives inordinate weight to a handful of people who, supposedly, know precisely how everyone else can best manage their finances. This concentration of power is exactly why policymakers should fear *the current system*, because no group of people can possibly have such knowledge. Moreover, as the foregoing narrative has shown, history is littered with evidence that the current approach does not work—it produces a fragile system that perpetuates more of the same kinds of failures witnessed for more than a century. The financial system, like the rest of the economy, should be based on the time-tested principle that free markets work better than government-directed economic activity.

The good news for policymakers is that many Americans broadly oppose the long-term regulatory trends in US financial markets and support a more market-based approach. For instance, the Cato Institute's national survey of Americans' views about the financial sector finds that 78 percent of Americans think regulations too often fail to have their intended effect, and 73 percent negatively rate government regulators for protecting consumers and investors from unethical business practices.[487] Of those surveyed, 77 percent do not think that regulators help financial firms make better business decisions, 68 percent do not think regulators help financial firms make better decisions about how much risk to take, and only 29 percent believe regulators are doing a good or excellent job overseeing the banking and financial industry. According to the survey, most Americans believe that regulation should serve two primary functions: 64 percent believe regulation should protect consumers from fraud, and 53 percent believe that regulation should help ensure that financial institutions fulfill obligations to their account holders. In contrast, fewer Americans support the types of government-directed activities that exist in the current system. Only 16 percent, for instance, support government regulations that restrict access to risky financial products, and only 13 percent support government regulations that prevent consumers from making bad decisions.

For decades, Congress has empowered regulators to manage private sector risks and mitigate losses, all in the name of preventing financial turmoil from spreading to the rest of the economy. It hasn't worked. The good news, though, is that it appears most Americans are open to a different approach.

Acknowledgments

We would like to thank Whitney Michel for reading so many drafts, Gabriella Beaumont Smith for making so many helpful suggestions, and Jerome Famularo and Nick Thielman for their valuable research assistance. We would also like to thank Ivan Osorio, Nick Anthony, Simone Shenny Berdahl, Andrew Berdahl, Chad Davis, Jai Kedia, and Ann Rulon.

Notes

CHAPTER 1

Box 1.1

a. Norbert Michel, "The Myth of Financial Market Deregulation," Heritage Foundation Backgrounder no. 3094, April 26, 2016.

b. Based on authors' analysis of *Federal Register*. Norbert Michel and Tamara Skinner, "The Popular Narrative about Financial Deregulation Is Wrong," *Daily Signal*, July 29, 2016.

c. These dollar figures are in constant 2000 dollars. Veronique de Rugy and Melinda Warren, "The Incredible Growth of the Regulators' Budget," Mercatus Center Working Paper no. 08-36, September 2008, pp. 3–4.

d. This figure updates the estimate provided in Diane Katz, "The Massive Federal Credit Racket," Heritage Foundation Backgrounder no. 3179, February 14, 2017. It primarily includes obligations related to Fannie Mae and Freddie Mac, the Federal Home Loan Banks, the Federal Deposit Insurance Corporation, and multiple federal credit programs.

e. These figures include both single-family and multifamily MBS. Securities Industry and Financial Markets Association, "US MBS: Issuance, Trading Volume, Outstanding," October 13, 2021; Ginnie Mae, "Issuance Summary," March 2021.

f. Board of Governors of the Federal Reserve System, "Assets: Securities Held Outright: Mortgage-Backed Securities: Wednesday Level," retrieved from FRED, Federal Reserve Bank of St. Louis, June 26, 2022.

CHAPTER 2

1. Eric Foner, *Give Me Liberty! An American History* (New York: W. W. Norton, 2019), p. 224.

2. Foner, *Give Me Liberty!*, p. 302.

3. Indeed, even the so-called Panic of 1837 defies a simple explanation. For a detailed account of the many different events that have come to be known as the Panic of 1837, see Jessica M. Leeper, *The Many Panics of 1837: People, Politics, and the Creation of a Transatlantic Financial Crisis* (New York: Cambridge University Press, 2013).

4. One of the first banks to form was the Bank of New York. It formed in 1784, but it failed to obtain a state charter until 1791. Peter L. Rousseau and Richard Sylla, "Emerging Financial Markets and Early US Growth," *Explorations in Economic History* 42, no. 1 (2005): 4.

5. Benjamin J. Klebaner, "State-Chartered American Commercial Banks, 1781–1801," *Business History Review* 52, no. 4 (1979): 529.

6. Klebaner, "State-Chartered American Commercial Banks," p. 529 (emphasis added).

7. Necessarily, this estimate includes only those state banks that reported their paid-in capital, so it is likely a low estimate. Rousseau and Sylla, "Emerging Financial Markets," p. 5. Also see J. Van Fenstermaker, "The Statistics of American Commercial Banking, 1782–1818," *Journal of Economic History* 25, no. 3 (1965): 400–413.

8. Howard Bodenhorn, "Antebellum Banking in the United States," EH.Net Encyclopedia, ed. Robert Whaples, March 26, 2008. Even more remarkable, much of this growth occurred before industrialization was entrenched throughout the United States. See Matthew Jaremski, "National Banking's Role in U.S. Industrialization, 1850–1900," National Bureau of Economic Research Working Paper no. 18789, February 2013.

9. Rousseau and Sylla, "Emerging Financial Markets," p. 5.

10. Charles W. Calomiris and Stephen H. Haber, *Fragile by Design: The Political Origins of Banking Crises and Scarce Credit* (Princeton, NJ: Princeton University Press, 2014), p. 159.

11. Edwin J. Perkins, *American Public Finance and Financial Services, 1700–1815* (Columbus: Ohio State University Press, 1994), p. 400.

12. Perkins, *American Public Finance*, pp. 313–14. The first document predated the better-known Buttonwood Agreement, signed by 24 stockbrokers on May 17, 1792. See Intercontinental Exchange Inc., "The History of NYSE," 2023.

13. Perkins, *American Public Finance*, p. 314. Options contracts were created as far back as the fourth century BCE. Geoffrey Poitras, "The Early History of Option

Contracts," in *Vinzenz Bronzin's Option Pricing Models*, ed. Wolfgang Hafner and Heinz Zimmermann (Berlin and Heidelberg: Springer, 2009), pp. 487–518.

14. Perkins, *American Public Finance*, pp. 314–15. According to Perkins, such contracts had been unenforceable under English law since 1734, but investors continued to use them in London anyway, which is what occurred in the New York market. Short selling dates to the late 1500s in the Dutch Republic, and the flamboyant Isaac Le Maire even used short selling to drive down the price of companies he wanted to purchase, a technique now known as a "bear raid." See Tom Taulli, *The Streetsmart Guide to Short Selling: Techniques the Pros Use to Profit in Any Market* (New York: McGraw-Hill, 2003), p. 1. Although the 1792 price collapse is sometimes referred to as America's first stock market crash, evidence suggests the decline was isolated to the New York market and was more of a "market reversal" than a "crash."

15. Rousseau and Sylla, "Emerging Financial Markets," p. 6.

16. Rousseau and Sylla, "Emerging Financial Markets," p. 6.

17. Perkins, *American Public Finance*, p. 317.

18. Rousseau and Sylla, "Emerging Financial Markets," p. 7. For general information on each of these markets, see Stuart Banner, "The Origin of the New York Stock Exchange, 1791–1860," *Journal of Legal Studies* 27, no. 1 (1998): 113–40; and Richard Sylla, "Financial Foundations: Public Credit, the National Bank, and Securities Markets," in *Founding Choices: American Economic Policy in the 1790s*, ed. Douglas Irwin and Richard Sylla (Chicago: University of Chicago Press, 2010), pp. 59–88.

19. Rousseau and Sylla, "Emerging Financial Markets," pp. 8–9.

20. Richard Sylla, "U.S. Securities Markets and the Banking System, 1790–1840," Federal Reserve Bank of St. Louis *Review*, May–June 1998.

21. Sylla, "U.S. Securities Markets," p. 93.

22. Sylla, "U.S. Securities Markets," p. 94.

23. George D. Green, *Finance and Economic Development in the Old South: Louisiana Banking, 1804–1861* (Stanford, CA: Stanford University Press, 1972), p. 5. Research also suggests that the banking systems in the "older" southern states (Georgia, Louisiana, North Carolina, South Carolina, and Virginia) were far superior to those in the "newer" southern states, because the systems financed broader commercial activities and because those states did not make banking a state-run monopoly. See Larry Schweikart, *Banking in the American South from the Age of Jackson to Reconstruction* (Baton Rouge: Louisiana State University Press, 1987).

24. Green, *Finance and Economic Development in the Old South*, p. 5; Thomas E. Redard, "The Port of New Orleans: An Economic History, 1821–1860 (Volumes I and II) (Trade, Commerce, Slaves, Louisiana)" (PhD diss., Louisiana State University, 1985).

25. Green, *Finance and Economic Development in the Old South*, p. 61.

26. Perkins, *American Public Finance*, p. 317.

27. Perkins, *American Public Finance*, p. 321.

28. Richard Sylla, "Forgotten Men of Money: Private Bankers in Early U.S. History," *Journal of Economic History* 36, no. 1 (1976): 173–88; Bray Hammond, *Banks and Politics in America: From the Revolution to the Civil War* (Princeton, NJ: Princeton University Press, 1957), p. 626. Near the beginning of his book (p. 68), Hammond claims that the antebellum United States was "spotted with public banks and had no private ones, at least none of sufficient importance to leave evidence that they existed." Yet near the end of the same book (p. 625), he claims that it is "likely" that "areas where banking was prohibited were all the time served more than they realized by incorporated banks elsewhere and by unincorporated banks in their own midst."

29. Sylla, "Forgotten Men of Money," pp. 180–81.

30. Sylla, "Forgotten Men of Money," p. 175. The use of deposits as bank money dates to at least the 15th century. Abbott Payson Usher, "The Origins of Banking: The Primitive Bank of Deposit, 1200–1600," *Economic History Review* 4, no. 4 (1934): 399–428.

31. Sylla, "Forgotten Men of Money," p. 177. In 1856, the US treasury secretary James Guthrie reported, "The combined capital in chartered and unchartered banks being over $460,000,000, proves that banking is a favorite as well as a profitable business, and does not need chartered privileges to generate or protect it." US Secretary of the Treasury, "Report on Banks" (1856), 34th Cong., 1st sess., House Executive Document no. 102, p. 1 (cited in Richard Sylla, "The Forgotten Private Banker," April 1, 1995, Foundation for Economic Education.

32. Sylla, "Forgotten Men of Money," p. 179.

33. For instance, according to the Economic History Association, per capita income in the United States ranked fifth in the world by 1820, "falling roughly thirty percent below the leaders (United Kingdom and the Netherlands), but still two-to-three times better off than the poorest sections of the globe." Richard Steckel, "A History of the Standard of Living in the United States," EH.Net Encyclopedia, ed. Robert Whaples, July 21, 2002.

34. Rousseau and Sylla, "Emerging Financial Markets," p. 14.

35. Sylla, "U.S. Securities Markets," p. 97.

36. Francisco J. Buera, Joseph P. Kaboski, and Yongseok Shin, "Finance and Development: A Tale of Two Sectors," *American Economic Review* 101, no. 5 (2011): 1964–2002.

37. Buera, Kaboski, and Shin, "A Tale of Two Sectors."

38. Robert G. King and Ross Levine, "Finance and Growth: Schumpeter Might Be Right," *Quarterly Journal of Economics* 108, no. 3 (1993): 719.

39. King and Levine, "Finance and Growth," p. 719.

40. Raghuram G. Rajan and Luigi Zingales, "Financial Dependence and Growth," *American Economic Review* 88, no. 3 (1998): 559–86.

41. Rajan and Zingales, "Financial Dependence and Growth."

42. Rajan and Zingales, "Financial Dependence and Growth," p. 559.

43. Lin-Manuel Miranda, "Cabinet Battle #1," *Hamilton*, Act 2.

44. Indeed, these themes, including the general distrust of financial markets, are not exclusive to the United States. See Peter M. Garber, "Famous First Bubbles," *Journal of Economic Perspectives* 4, no. 2 (1990): 35–54; and Hammond, *Banks and Politics in America*.

45. Richard Brookhiser, *Alexander Hamilton, American* (New York: Touchstone, 2000), p. 84.

46. Brookhiser, *Alexander Hamilton*, p. 84.

47. Brookhiser, *Alexander Hamilton*, p. 84. The full letter is found in *The Papers of Alexander Hamilton*, vol. 5, ed. Harold C. Syrett (Charlottesville: University of Virginia Press, 2011), p. 465, digital edition.

48. Brookhiser, *Alexander Hamilton*, pp. 84, 86.

49. Brookhiser, *Alexander Hamilton*, p. 85.

50. Brookhiser, *Alexander Hamilton*, p. 90.

51. Brookhiser, *Alexander Hamilton*, p. 90.

52. Brookhiser, *Alexander Hamilton*, p. 90. As Brookhiser explains (p. 87), Hamilton was not proposing a strict replication of the Bank of England. He wanted the US bank to be run by private individuals, and he believed that public control would "corrode the vitals" of the bank's credit. He also wrote, "The keen, steady and … magnetic" self-interest of private proprietors was "the only security that can always be relied upon for a careful and prudent administration." Hamilton also argued that the bank, not the government, should issue money. He wrote, "The wisdom of the government will be shown in never trusting itself with the use of so seducing and dangerous an expedient."

53. Brookhiser, *Alexander Hamilton*, p. 86.

54. Brookhiser, *Alexander Hamilton*, p. 86.

55. Brookhiser, *Alexander Hamilton*, p. 87.

56. Brookhiser, *Alexander Hamilton*, p. 87.

57. The system was crisis-prone because (among other shortcomings) it severely restricted branch banking. Calomiris and Haber, *Fragile by Design*, pp. 153–54.

58. Aside from Jefferson, Jackson, and Lincoln, the list also includes lesser-known politicians such as William Jennings Bryan and Henry B. Steagall (the namesake of the 1933 Glass-Steagall Act that "separated" commercial and investment banking). Calomiris and Haber, *Fragile by Design*, p. 157.

59. Calomiris and Haber, *Fragile by Design*, p. 158; Susan Hoffman, *Politics and Banking: Ideas, Public Policy, and the Creation of Financial Institutions* (Baltimore: Johns Hopkins University Press, 2001), pp. 183–85.

60. Hoffman, *Politics and Banking*, pp. 183–85.

61. Hoffman, *Politics and Banking*, pp. 183–85.

62. Hoffman, *Politics and Banking*, p. 107.

63. Hoffman, *Politics and Banking*, pp. 106–7. For a general discussion, see Francis A. Walker, "The Free Coinage of Silver," *Journal of Political Economy* 1, no. 2 (1893): 163–78.

64. Hoffman, *Politics and Banking*, pp. 107–8. In 2023, after nearly 100 years without any official commodity money in the United States, it is difficult to convey how momentous this change really was. But for many, it was a complete rejection of their previous view that gold was the "natural" form of money.

65. In 1873, Congress officially took the United States off the bimetallic system when it officially demonetized silver. By 1875, the supply of silver had increased, but it had not circulated for generations so there was no provision at the US Mint for minting silver. Nonetheless, at that time, it would have been profitable to sell silver at the prewar legal ratio.

66. Bimetallism and the "free silver movement" were originally popularized by several minor third parties, including the Populist Party, the American Bimetallic League, and the American Bimetallic Party. Samuel Decanio, "Populism, Paranoia, and the Politics of Free Silver," *Studies in American Political Development* 25, no. 1 (2011): 2.

67. Hoffman, *Politics and Banking*, p. 108. For broader context on the monetary and financial conflicts of the era, see Irwin Unger, *The Greenback Era: A Social and Political History of American Finance, 1865–1879* (Princeton, NJ: Princeton University Press, 1964).

68. Hoffman, *Politics and Banking*, pp. 108–9; Walker, "The Free Coinage of Silver"; Milton Friedman and Anna Schwartz, *A Monetary History of the United States, 1867–1960* (Princeton, NJ: Princeton University Press, 1963), pp. 113–19.

69. Hoffman, *Politics and Banking*, p. 111.

70. "Bryan's 'Cross of Gold' Speech: Mesmerizing the Masses," Official Proceedings of the Democratic National Convention Held in Chicago, July 7, 8, 9, 10, and 11, 1896 (Logansport, IN, 1896), pp. 226–34. Reprinted in *The Annals of America*, vol. 12, *1895–1904: Populism, Imperialism, and Reform* (Chicago: Encyclopedia Britannica, 1968), pp. 100–105.

71. "Bryan's 'Cross of Gold' Speech."

72. "Bryan's 'Cross of Gold' Speech."

73. Hoffman, *Politics and Banking*, p. 113. Bryan's own descriptions add valuable context. William Jennings Bryan, "The Election of 1900," *North American Review* 171, no. 529 (1900): 788–801.

74. Hoffman, *Politics and Banking*, p. 113.

75. Hoffman, *Politics and Banking*, p. 112.

76. George Selgin, "New York's Bank: The National Monetary Commission and the Founding of the Fed," Cato Institute Policy Analysis no. 793, June 21, 2016.

77. Selgin, "New York's Bank."

78. Selgin, "New York's Bank."

79. Selgin, "New York's Bank."

80. Selgin, "New York's Bank."

81. This point marked a major shift in American politics because, for the first time, the Democratic Party took an overall favorable view toward federal regulation and expansive government authority, even though the party retained its hostility toward "banks and concentrated economic power." Decanio, "The Politics of Free Silver," p. 2.

82. Selgin, "New York's Bank."

83. Hoffman, *Politics and Banking*, p. 168.

84. Hoffman, *Politics and Banking*, p. 168; Kathleen Day, *S & L Hell: The People and the Politics behind the $1 Trillion Savings and Loan Scandal* (New York: W. W. Norton, 1993), p. 42.

85. "Regulation of Stock Market Manipulation," *Yale Law Journal* 56, no. 3 (1947): 509–33.

86. "Regulation of Stock Market Manipulation," p. 509, fn 1.

87. Separately, a popular view of banking crises is that they often result from prior bank lending "manias," which are more likely in legally unrestricted banking systems. Yet research suggests that this view is incorrect. George Selgin, "Bank Lending 'Manias' in Theory and History," *Journal of Financial Services Research* 6 (1992): 169–86.

88. Harold Bierman, "The 1929 Stock Market Crash," EH.Net Encyclopedia, ed, Robert Whaples, March 26, 2008.

89. Bierman, "1929 Stock Market Crash."

90. Bierman, "1929 Stock Market Crash."

91. Bierman, "1929 Stock Market Crash."

92. For instance, in his best-selling book *The Great Crash, 1929*, John Kenneth Galbraith writes: "Early in 1928, the nature of the boom changed. The mass escape into make-believe, so much a part of the true speculative orgy, started in earnest." Although it is easy to cast such an aspersion on a market bubble in hindsight, after the boom has ended, Galbraith never explains any objective criteria by which to measure such a "speculative orgy" relative to previous buying and selling. Galbraith, *The Great Crash, 1929* (New York: Houghton Mifflin Harcourt, 1954), p. 11.

93. Though there appears to be no single cause of the Depression, academic research shows that the Depression followed multiple economic shocks that

occurred both before and after the 1929 stock market crash, and that any wealth effects from the market collapse were small. Rather than the stock market collapse itself, more likely culprits for what caused the Depression include several real shocks, such as going off the gold exchange standard—which led to a drain of bank deposits that caused bank failures—and protectionist trade policies such as the Smoot-Hawley tariffs, some of the highest import tariffs in the history of the United States. Robert F. Bruner and Scott C. Miller, "The Great Crash of 1929: A Look Back after 90 Years," *Journal of Applied Corporate Finance* 31, no. 4 (2019): 43–58; Kris Mitchener, Kevin O'Rourke, and Kirsten Wandschneider, "The Smoot-Hawley Trade War," *Economic Journal* 132, no. 647 (2022): 2500–33.

94. Calomiris and Haber, *Fragile by Design*, p. 191.

95. Julia Maues, "Banking Act of 1933 (Glass-Steagall)," Federal Reserve History webpage, November 22, 2013.

96. Hoffman, *Politics and Banking*, p. 171. Building and loan associations, depicted in the 1946 film *It's a Wonderful Life*, were started on notions of mutual self-help, whereby individuals held shares in the institutions and had both borrowing privileges and the right to dividends. In the 1880s, *national* building and loans emerged, with riskier business models, and they imploded after a major real estate downturn associated with the depression of 1893. In the eyes of the local associations, the national building and loans had besmirched the industry. David Price and John Walter, "It's a Wonderful Loan: A Short History of Building and Loan Associations," Federal Reserve Bank of Richmond Economic Brief no. 19-01, January 2019.

97. Hoffman, *Politics and Banking*, p. 172.

98. Hoffman, *Politics and Banking*, p. 172.

99. Hoffman, *Politics and Banking*, p. 182.

100. Hoffman, *Politics and Banking*, p. 182. Some credit unions still use this idea in their promotional material. For example, TruChoice Federal Credit Union's website states, "Credit unions were founded on the principles of economic democracy—where every member has equal ownership and one vote." TruChoice Federal Credit Union, "Benefits of Credit Unions over Big Banks," March 4, 2024.

101. Hoffman, *Politics and Banking*, pp. 191–93.

102. Bergengren successfully advocated for the passage of the Federal Credit Union Act and the creation of the Credit Union National Association. Hoffman, *Politics and Banking*, p. 194.

103. Hoffman, *Politics and Banking*, p. 189.

104. A 1996 law review article about derivatives regulation notes, "In the popular press and to the average citizen, 'derivatives,' much like speculation, has become a dirty word, hindering informed discussion." Roberta Romano, "A Thumbnail Sketch of Derivative Securities and Their Regulation," *Maryland Law Review* 55, no. 1 (1996): 4–5.

105. Norbert Michel, "The Glass–Steagall Act: Unraveling the Myth," Heritage Foundation Backgrounder no. 3104, April 28, 2016.

106. Another underappreciated fact is that the Glass-Steagall separation only applied to US banks' domestic operations. By the 1980s, the largest US banks were particularly active in international markets. For instance, the top 30 Eurobond underwriters in 1985 were US bank affiliates. George J. Benston, *The Separation of Commercial and Investment Banking* (New York: Oxford University Press, 1990), p. 10.

107. Benston, *Separation of Commercial and Investment Banking*, p. 41.

108. Michel, "The Glass–Steagall Act."

109. James Anderson, "Some Say Occupy Wall Street Did Nothing. It Changed Us More Than We Think," *Time*, November 15, 2021.

110. Alex Howe, "10 Demands Being Made by the Wall Street Protesters," *Business Insider*, September 28, 2011. Also see "Elizabeth Warren on Glass-Steagall in 2013," YouTube video, July 12, 2013, https://www.youtube.com/watch?v=X-POblwXtzNs.

111. Norbert Michel, *Why Shadow Banking Didn't Cause the Financial Crisis: And Why Regulating Contagion Won't Help* (Washington: Cato Institute, 2022).

112. As of January 2007, for instance, 67 of the 127 sponsors rated by Moody's Investors Service were commercial banks, accounting for 74 percent of outstanding asset-backed commercial paper ($911 billion). See Viral V. Acharya, Philipp Schnabl, and Gustavo Suarez, "Securitization without Risk Transfer," *Journal of Financial Economics* 107, no. 3 (2013): 515–36.

113. Gillian Tett, *Fool's Gold* (New York: Free Press, 2009), pp. 23–71, 97.

CHAPTER 3

114. In fact, so-called excessive speculation has been a popular explanation for financial crises for hundreds of years, dating to (at least) the 17th century. Three of the oldest examples are the Dutch Tulip Mania (1634), the Mississippi Bubble (1717), and the South Sea Bubble (1720). See Peter M. Garber, "Famous First Bubbles," *Journal of Economic Perspectives* 4, no. 2 (1990): 35–54.

115. John Bellamy Foster, "The Financialization of Capitalism," *Monthly Review*, April 1, 2007. Summarizing several authors' arguments, including those of Paul A. Baran, Paul Sweezy, and Harry Magdoff, Foster claims, "Stagnation and enormous financial speculation emerged as symbiotic aspects of the same deep-seated, irreversible economic impasse."

116. Senator Marco Rubio, *American Investment in the 21st Century*, May 15, 2019, p. 4.

117. Senator Marco Rubio, "Marco Rubio: We Need to Invest in America Again," *Washington Examiner*, May 13, 2019.

118. The risk for any portfolio of financial assets is less than the average of the individual assets' risks, provided the assets' returns are not perfectly, positively correlated. This is known as the diversification effect, where adding assets that are not perfectly, positively correlated to any portfolio reduces its overall risk (variability in returns). Thus, all else being constant, a larger number of financial assets allow for greater diversification of risk. Stephen A. Ross, Randolph W. Westerfield, and Jeffrey Jaffe, *Corporate Finance*, 5th ed. (Boston: Irwin/McGraw-Hill, 1999), p. 239.

119. Rubio, *American Investment in the 21st Century*, p. 40.

120. For a more detailed discussion of these functions and benefits, see Tony Saunders, Marcia M. Cornett, and Otgo Erhemjamts, *Financial Markets and Institutions*, 8th ed. (New York: McGraw Hill, 2022), pp. 11–16.

121. In the 1990s, Southwest Airlines pioneered the use of derivatives to hedge jet fuel expenses. Southwest Airlines Co., "The Southwest Jet Fuel Hedge Strategy," 2021; Robert Brooks, "A Life Cycle View of Enterprise Risk Management: The Case of Southwest Airlines Jet Fuel Hedging," *Journal of Financial Education* 38, no. 3–4 (2012): 33–45.

122. Michael S. Rozeff, "Rothbard on Fractional Reserve Banking: A Critique," *Independent Review* 14, no. 4 (2010): 497–512.

123. "Statistics at a Glance," Federal Deposit Insurance Corporation, Second Quarter, 2023.

124. Technically, these institutions, as well as commercial banks, fall under the broader category of *depository institution*. Title 12, § 3201, of the *United States Code* defines a depository institution as "a commercial bank, a savings bank, a trust company, a savings and loan association, a building and loan association, a homestead association, a cooperative bank, an industrial bank, or a credit union."

125. Federal Deposit Insurance Corporation, "Statistics at a Glance," Second Quarter, 2023.

126. National Credit Union Administration, "Quarterly Credit Union Data Summary," Fourth Quarter, 2022.

127. Before the 1980s, insurance companies were one of the larger sources of funds for home mortgages in the United States. Matthew Wells, "A Short History of Long-Term Mortgages," Federal Reserve Bank of Richmond *Econ Focus*, First Quarter 2023, pp. 18–22. Wells notes: "The National Bank Act of 1864 barred commercial banks from writing mortgages, but life insurance companies and mutual savings banks were active lenders. They were, however, heavily regulated and often barred from lending across state lines or beyond certain distances from their location."

128. American Council of Life Insurers, *Life Insurers Fact Book 2022* (Washington: American Council of Life Insurers, 2022), p. 3.

129. Michele Wong, "Growth in U.S. Insurance Industry's Cash and Invested Assets Declines to 1.3% at Year-End 2022," National Association of Insurance

Commissioners, Capital Markets Special Report, 2022, p. 2. These totals are not necessarily all invested in primary-market securities, but many insurance companies also own investment companies that serve as financial intermediaries. In 2019, for instance, insurance companies managed 4 percent of the mutual fund industry's assets. The mutual fund industry's total assets in 2019 were $17.7 trillion. Saunders, Cornett, and Erhemjamts, *Financial Markets and Institutions*, pp. 538–39.

130. Mordor Intelligence, *Investment Banking Market (2024–2029)* (Hyderabad, India: Mordor Intelligence, 2023).

131. "Investment Banking Scorecard," *Wall Street Journal*, Moneybeat, 2024.

132. Office of the Advocate for Small Business Capital Formation, US Securities and Exchange Commission, "What Is a Broker-Dealer?" (webpage); 15 US Code § 78c(a)(4), (5).

133. For a description of the role of an investment bank in a securities distribution, see Marc Levinson, *Guide to Financial Markets: Why They Exist and How They Work* (New York: Public Affairs, 2018), p. 163 (describing the role of an investment bank in a securities distribution).

134. Financial Industry Regulatory Authority, *2023 FINRA Industry Snapshot* (Washington: FINRA, 2023), p. 13. All broker-dealers are required to be members of a self-regulatory organization, which sets standards, conducts examinations, and enforces rules regarding its members. Self-regulatory organizations, such as FINRA and the national stock exchanges, are regulated by the Securities and Exchange Commission.

135. Financial Industry Regulatory Authority, *2023 FINRA Industry Snapshot*, p. 6.

136. Katie Kolchin, Justyna Podziemska, and Dan Song, *Capital Markets Fact Book, 2023* (Washington and New York: Securities Industry and Financial Markets Association, 2023), pp. 96–97.

137. Kolchin, Podziemska, and Song, *Capital Markets Factbook, 2023*, p. 98; Mark Schoeff Jr., "Number of Registered Reps and Brokerages Declined Again in 2020: Finra," *Investment News*, May 25, 2021; Investment Adviser Association (IAA), *Investment Adviser Industry Snapshot 2023* (Washington: IAA, 2023), p. 20.

138. In 2022, 312,317 registered representatives were dually registered as broker-dealer and investment adviser representatives versus 80,977 that were registered only as investment adviser representatives. IAA, *Investment Adviser Industry Snapshot 2023*, p. 20. Large firms tend to be dually registered, but most individual advisers are dually registered through separate, affiliated entities. IAA, *Investment Adviser Industry Snapshot 2023*, p. 76.

139. IAA, *Investment Adviser Industry Snapshot 2023*, pp. 28–29.

140. Kolchin, Podziemska, and Song, *Capital Markets Factbook 2023*, pp. 97, 102 (giving the total as 32,500 versus giving the total of SEC and state-registered investment advisers as 40,848); IAA, *Investment Adviser Industry Snapshot 2023*, p. 18 (noting

that there are 15,114 SEC-registered investment advisers and 17,406 state-registered investment advisers).

141. SEC-registered advisers employ 366,943 investment adviser representatives (p. 18), whereas state-registered advisers employ 26,351 representatives (p. 2). IAA, *Investment Adviser Industry Snapshot 2023*.

142. IAA, *Investment Adviser Industry Snapshot 2023*, p. 25.

143. Kolchin, Podziemska, and Song, *Capital Markets Factbook, 2023*, p. 97. The number of SEC-registered firms has increased in 20 of the past 22 years. Registrations declined in 2010 and 2011 when the minimum size threshold for SEC registration increased to $100 million from $25 million in assets under management. IAA, *Investment Adviser Industry Snapshot 2023*), p. 14.

144. IAA, *Investment Adviser Industry Snapshot 2023*, pp. 12, 26.

145. 15 US Code § 80a-3.

146. World Bank, "Listed Domestic Companies, Total—United States," World Bank Indicators database, accessed February 29, 2024.

147. Nicole Goodkind, "America Has Lost Half Its Public Companies since the 1990s. Here's Why," CNN Business, June 9, 2023.

148. Jay Ritter, "Initial Public Offerings: Updated Statistics," University of Florida, February 23, 2024, table 8. The total number of IPOs can vary substantially from year to year based, in part, on economic conditions. But the long-term trend since the 1990s has been a substantially lower number of IPOs.

149. The OTC market involves the process of trading securities via a broker-dealer network, as opposed to a centralized exchange. It is estimated that approximately three times as many publicly available stocks trade over the counter as trade on organized exchanges. Levinson, *Guide to Financial Markets*, p. 178. A number of networks operate in the OTC market, many of which have their own standards for including securities for trading. OTC trading is not limited to shares of stock offered to the public; lots of different types of securities, such as nonpublic company stock, bonds, and derivatives, trade over the counter. Stocks traded in the OTC market are generally less liquid, owing to lower trading volumes, and trading on the OTC market is generally less efficient as a result. OTC stocks are also generally less regulated than those that trade on the stock exchanges—which have their own listing standards in addition to SEC regulation. As a result, OTC stocks are generally understood to be more speculative and riskier.

150. Kolchin, Podziemska, and Song, *Capital Markets Factbook, 2023*, p. 7.

151. Kolchin, Podziemska, and Song, *Capital Markets Factbook, 2023*, p. 7.

152. Kolchin, Podziemska, and Song, *Capital Markets Factbook, 2023*, p. 59.

153. Board of Governors of the Federal Reserve System, "Survey of Consumer Finances, 1989–2022: Stock Holdings by All Families, last updated November 2, 2023; Hannah Miao, "More Americans than Ever Own Stocks," *Wall Street Journal*, December 18, 2023.

154. Kolchin, Podziemska, and Song, *Capital Markets Factbook, 2023*, p. 77.

155. Kolchin, Podziemska, and Song, *Capital Markets Factbook. 2023*, p. 75.

156. Although fixed-income trading is still conducted manually, often over the phone, digital trading—and its associated transparency—has increased substantially. The prevalence of electronic trading, and the networks over which it occurs, vary according to the type of debt instrument that is being traded. Kevin McPartland and Katie Kolchin, *Understanding Fixed-Income Markets in 2023* (Stamford, CT: Coalition Greenwich and Securities Industry and Financial Markets Association, 2023), pp. 10–14. The market with the most electronic trading is the one for US Treasuries, where, in 2022, two-thirds of trading was done electronically. McPartland and Kolchin, *Understanding Fixed-Income Markets*, p. 12.

157. For example, approximately 66,000 corporate bonds are available to trade, and the municipal bond market has about one million tradable bonds. Not only are many of these bonds bought as long-term investments that the investor plans to hold until maturity, the sheer volume and diversity of bonds available make it less likely that any particular issuance has substantial liquidity. McPartland and Kolchin, *Understanding Fixed-Income Markets*, p. 15. Conversely, in 2022, an average of $590 billion of US Treasury bonds were traded each day, with 65 percent of that volume traded electronically. McPartland and Kolchin, *Understanding Fixed-Income Markets*, p. 5.

158. Kolchin, Podziemska, and Song, *Capital Markets Factbook, 2023*, p. 7.

159. Kolchin, Podziemska, and Song, *Capital Markets Factbook, 2023*, p. 49.

160. McPartland and Kolchin, *Understanding Fixed-Income Markets*, p. 15.

161. Richard G. Anderson and Charles S. Gascon, "The Commercial Paper Market, the Fed, and the 2007–2009 Financial Crisis," Federal Reserve Bank of St. Louis *Review*, November–December 2009, p. 589. Also see Richard T. Selden, "Four Decades of Change in the Commercial Paper Market," in *Trends and Cycles in the Commercial Paper Market*, ed. Richard T. Selden (Cambridge, MA: National Bureau of Economic Research, 1963), pp. 6–30.

162. Lloyd B. Thomas, *Money, Banking, and Financial Markets* (Mason, OH: Thomson/South-Western, 2006), pp. 52–53; Charles W. Calomiris, Charles P. Himmelberg, and Paul Wachtel, "Commercial Paper, Corporate Finance, and the Business Cycle: A Microeconomic Perspective," *Carnegie-Rochester Conference Series on Public Policy* 42 (1995): 205.

163. The short-term maturity is by choice of investors and issuers, not because of regulatory requirements. Anderson and Gascon, "The Commercial Paper Market."

164. Viral V. Acharya, Philipp Schnabl, and Gustavo Suarez, "Securitization without Risk Transfer," *Journal of Financial Economics* 107, no. 3 (2013): 519–20.

165. Board of Governors of the Federal Reserve System, "Commercial Paper Outstanding," retrieved from FRED, Federal Reserve Bank of St. Louis,

January 1, 2024. The decline from 2007 is almost entirely attributable to a reduction in the amount of ABCP issued after the drop in value during the 2008
financial crisis. Incidentally, the amount of ABCP issued increased dramatically
just before the crisis (in 2005) and has never returned to the levels outstanding
before 2005. Acharya, Schnabl, and Suarez, "Securitization without Risk Transfer," p. 518; Board of Governors of the Federal Reserve System, "Asset-Backed
Commercial Paper Outstanding," retrieved from FRED, Federal Reserve Bank
of St. Louis, October 24, 2023.

166. Board of Governors of the Federal Reserve System, "Commercial and
Industrial Loans, All Commercial Banks," retrieved from FRED, Federal Reserve
Bank of St. Louis, January 1, 2024.

167. Viktoria Baklanova, Adam Copeland, and Rebecca McCaughrin, "Reference Guide to U.S. Repo and Securities Lending Markets," Federal Reserve
Bank of New York Staff Report no. 740, December 2015, p. 5.

168. SIFMA Research, *The US Repo Markets: A Chart Book* (Washington:
Securities Industry and Financial Markets Association, 2022.

169. SIFMA Research, *The US Repo Markets*, p. 6.

170. Lending or borrowing on an overnight basis is attractive because it min-
imizes both interest rate and collateral risk, a feature that can be especially important to anyone with a large surplus of cash or securities.

171. Ralf R. Meisenzahl, "The Federal Reserve's Overnight and Term
Reverse Repurchase Agreement Operations in the Financial Accounts of the United States," FEDS Notes, March 24, 2015.

172. SIFMA Research, "US Repo Market Fact Sheet," January 2021.

173. International Capital Markets Association, "What Types of Asset Are
Used as Collateral in the Repo Market?," 2021; SIFMA Research, "US Repo Market Fact Sheet"; SIFMA, "Repo Market Fact Sheet," 2014; Viktoria Baklanova
et al., "The U.S. Bilateral Repo Market: Lessons from a New Survey," Office of
Financial Research Brief no. 16-01, US Department of the Treasury, January 13,
2016.

174. Thomas, *Money, Banking, and Financial Markets*, pp. 52–53; Baklanova,
Copeland, and McCaughrin, "Reference Guide to U.S. Repo and Securities Lending Markets."

175. Viktoria Baklanova, Isaac Kuznits, and Trevor Tatum, "Primer: Money
Market Funds and the Repo Market," Division of Investment Management's Analytics Office of the US Securities and Exchange Commission, February 18, 2021.

176. The two major segments of the repo market are (a) the tri-party
repo market, where a clearing bank—either the Bank of New York Mellon
or JPMorganChase—provides settlement and collateral management services,
and (b) the bilateral repo market, where all repos are executed directly by the
counterparties (the borrowers and lenders). In both the tri-party and bilateral

repo market segments, some transactions are "cleared," meaning that the counterparties transfer risk to a third party—a clearing bank. David Bowman et al., "The Cleared Bilateral Repo Market and Proposed Repo Benchmark Rates," FEDS Notes, February 27, 2017.

177. "Computer Leases Back Financing by Sperry," *New York Times*, February 12, 1985. Also see Alan P. Murray, "Has Securitization Increased Risk to the Financial System?," *Business Economics* 36, no. 1 (2001): 63–67.

178. Murray, "Has Securitization Increased Risk to the Financial System?," p. 63.

179. Nicola Cetorelli and Stavros Peristiani, "The Role of Banks in Asset Securitization," Federal Reserve Bank of New York *Economic Policy Review*, July 2012, p. 58. See also Melanie L. Fein, "The Shadow Banking Charade," February 15, 2013.

180. Cetorelli and Peristiani, "Role of Banks in Asset Securitization," p. 58.

181. Mutual funds are also known as open-end funds because they can issue unlimited new shares, priced daily on their net asset value. This differs from closed-end funds, which have a fixed number of shares, the prices of which are determined according to supply and demand, not according to the fund's net asset value. Closed-end funds are less popular than mutual funds; closed-end funds held a total of $252 billion in assets at the end of 2022. More than 60 percent of closed-end funds are bond funds. Sean Collins et al., *2023 Investment Company Fact Book: A Review of Trends and Activities in the Investment Company Industry* (Washington: Investment Company Institute, 2023), p. 62.

182. Kolchin, Podziemska, and Song, *Capital Markets Factbook, 2023*, p. 69.

183. Collins et al., *2023 Investment Company Fact Book*, p. 37.

184. Although there has been some variation, US mutual funds have held more than $20 trillion in net assets since 2019. Collins et al., *2023 Investment Company Fact Book*, p. 68.

185. Collins et al., *2023 Investment Company Fact Book*, p. 34.

186. The popularity of index products is not limited to mutual funds. Equity index exchange-traded funds have attracted nearly three times the net inflows of equity index mutual funds since 2013. Collins et al., *2023 Investment Company Fact Book*.

187. Collins et al., *2023 Investment Company Fact Book*, p. 47.

188. John J. Brennan et al., *Report of the Money Market Working Group* (Washington: Investment Company Institute, 2009), p. 141.

189. Thomas, *Money, Banking, and Financial Markets*, pp. 81–84.

190. Baklanova, Kuznits, and Tatum, "Primer: Money Market Funds and the Commercial Paper Market."

191. Baklanova, Kuznits, and Tatum, "Primer: Money Market Funds and the Repo Market."

192. Baklanova, Kuznits, and Tatum, "Primer: Money Market Funds and the Repo Market."

193. Because of interest-rate price controls in the banking sector, MMFs grew steadily throughout the 1970s, and in 1980, Congress passed the Depository Institutions Deregulation and Monetary Control Act to phase out the interest-rate caps by 1986. Congress also passed the Garn–St. Germain Depository Institutions Act in 1982, allowing depository institutions to offer money market deposit accounts that paid customers higher interest rates than those at the statutory caps. Betty R. Turner, "Markets for Money—Does the Garn–St. Germain Money Market Deposit Account Overcompete with Mutual Funds," *Vanderbilt Law Review* 36, no. 4 (1983): 1129–63.

194. Stefan Jacewitz and Haluk Unal, "Shadow Insurance? Money Market Fund Investors and Bank Sponsorship," *Review of Corporate Finance Studies* 11, no. 2 (2021): 5.

195. Other exchange-traded products, such as exchange-traded commodity funds or exchange-traded notes, are often referred to as ETFs, but they are subject to different regulatory structures from conventional ETFs.

196. Greg Iacurci, "3 Big Reasons Exchange-Traded Funds Went 'Mainstream' with Investors," CNBC, November 6, 2023.

197. Samara Cohen, "Seven Things to Know about Retail Investor ETF Activity," NASDAQ, May 24, 2023; "The US ETF Market: FAQs," Investment Company Institute, April 10, 2023.

198. Kolchin, Podziemska, and Song, *Capital Markets Factbook, 2023*, p. 72.

199. Kolchin, Podziemska, and Song, *Capital Markets Factbook, 2023*, p. 72.

200. "The US ETF Market: FAQs."

201. 15 US Code 15 § 80a-3(c)(1), (7).

202. IAA, *Investment Adviser Industry Snapshot 2023*, p. 61. The SEC places the number of private funds in the fourth quarter of 2022 at over 47,000. Staff of the Division of Investment Management's Analytics Office, Private Funds Statistics: SEC, January 2024, p. 4. The discrepancy is most likely due to the way in which the funds were measured; the SEC counts only private funds that are required to file a Form PF with the agency, which is required when they use SEC-registered investment advisers and have over $150 million in assets under management.

203. IAA, *Investment Adviser Industry Snapshot 2023*, p. 63.

204. IAA, *Investment Adviser Industry Snapshot 2023*, p. 62.

205. IAA, *Investment Adviser Industry Snapshot 2023*, p. 63.

206. IAA, *Investment Adviser Industry Snapshot 2023*, p. 62.

207. IAA, *Investment Adviser Industry Snapshot 2023*, p. 62.

208. IAA, *Investment Adviser Industry Snapshot 2023*, p. 63 (data for table 5F downloaded from online).

209. IAA, *Investment Adviser Industry Snapshot 2023*, p. 63.

210. IAA, *Investment Adviser Industry Snapshot 2023*, p. 63.

211. The exception is for an activist hedge fund, which seeks to exert influence on a company in which it is invested. But activist hedge funds accomplish their influence in a different way from private equity funds; hedge funds seek to acquire the smallest possible investment to achieve influence, often engaging in a campaign for corporate change through the shareholder governance process. Private equity funds, on the other hand, usually seek to acquire a majority ownership stake in the company with the goal of controlling the company's management and operations.

212. 15 US Code 15 § 80a-3(c)(1); 17 C.F.R. § 275.203(l)-1.

213. "Everyone Now Believes That Private Markets Are Better than Public Ones," *The Economist*, January 30, 2020.

214. Levinson, *Guide to Financial Markets*, p. 199 (noting that speculation is not unproductive—it is "essential to the smooth functioning of the market").

215. Kolchin, Podziemska, and Song, *Capital Markets Factbook, 2023*, p. 65.

216. Steven W. Poser, "Trends in Options Trading," NYSE, December 4, 2023. Retail options trading increased substantially during the COVID-19 pandemic in 2020 and has remained elevated since that time. Two possible reasons for the increase are retail options being an easier and cheaper way to access options trading (through trading apps) and an increase in the number of low-priced options. Editorial Staff, "Flash Friday: The Evolution of Retail Options Trading," *Traders Magazine*, June 16, 2023.

217. Alex Ferko, Scott Mixon, and Esen Onur, "Retail Trades in Futures Markets," Office of the Chief Economist, Commodity Futures Trading Commission, OCE Staff no. 2023-002, October 2023. Moreover, retail futures trading activity tends to be concentrated in certain instruments—specifically "micro" contracts on benchmark financial instruments, like the S&P 500. Ferko, Mixon, and Onur, "Retail Trades in Futures Markets," p. 26, table II.

218. Levinson, *Guide to Financial Markets*, p. 221.

219. Futures are also traded on currencies, with the first contracts launched in 1971. Leo Melamed, "The Birth of FX Futures," Chicago Mercantile Exchange.

220. "Volume by Region," Futures Industry Association ETD Tracker webpage, accessed March 1, 2024.

221. A swap execution facility is an electronic matching platform that brings together buyers and sellers of swap contracts, similar to an exchange.

222. Berkshire Hathaway, *2002 Annual Report* (Omaha, NE: Warren E. Buffett, 2003), p. 16.

CHAPTER 4

223. Glenn Greenwald, "Tucker Carlson on Global Populism, the Censor-ship-Industrial Regime, Israel/Ukraine, His New Network, & More," *System Update*, December 15, 2023. Also see Liz Wolfe, "Demonic Dollar Store," *Reason*, December 18, 2023.

224. William N. Goetzmann, *Money Changes Everything: How Finance Made Civilization Possible* (Princeton, NJ: Princeton University Press, 2016), p. 46.

225. Goetzmann, *Money Changes Everything*, p. 8.

226. Goetzmann, *Money Changes Everything*, p. 48.

227. Goetzmann, *Money Changes Everything*, p. 57.

228. Emil B. Berendt, "The Scholastic View on Usury and Economic Instabil-ity," *Journal of Economics, Theology and Religion* 3, no. 1–2 (2023): 25. As Berendt dis-cusses, usury laws existed in both Eastern and Western cultures through the millennia; John Houkes, *An Annotated Bibliography on the History of Usury and Interest from the Earliest Times through the Eighteenth Century* (Lewiston, NY: Edwin Mellen Press, 2004).

229. Goetzmann, *Money Changes Everything*, pp. 46–48.

230. Goetzmann, *Money Changes Everything*, p. 233.

231. Berendt, "Scholastic View on Usury," p. 25.

232. Goetzmann, *Money Changes Everything*, p. 233.

233. Berendt, "Scholastic View on Usury," p. 26.

234. Berendt, "Scholastic View on Usury," p. 26.

235. Goetzmann, *Money Changes Everything*, pp. 221–33. In *Summa Theologiae*, St. Thomas Aquinas wrote, "The Philosopher [Aristotle], led by natural reason, says that 'to make money by usury is exceedingly unnatural.'" Christopher Kaczor, "Did the Church Change Its Stance on Usury?," "Catholic Answers" website, July 1, 2006.

236. Goetzmann, *Money Changes Everything*, pp. 232–33.

237. Berendt, "Scholastic View on Usury," p. 28.

238. Brian McCall, "Unprofitable Lending: Modern Credit Regulation and the Lost Theory of Usury," *Cardozo Law Review* 30, no. 2 (2008): 566.

239. See, for example, Anne-Marie Bonneau, "21 Consumer Products You Can (Likely) Live Without," *Zero-Waste Chef* (blog), April 26, 2017.

240. Berendt, "Scholastic View on Usury," p. 28.

241. John T. Noonan Jr., *The Scholastic Analysis of Usury* (Cambridge, MA: Harvard University Press, 1957), p. 49.

242. Noonan, *Scholastic Analysis of Usury*, p. 49. Noonan maintains that Pope Innocent developed these arguments on his own.

243. Noonan, *Scholastic Analysis of Usury*, p. 377. Still, as modern prohibitions on interest in Islamic finance demonstrate, these anti-usury ideas have not com-pletely receded.

244. Lodewijk Petram, *The World's First Stock Exchange* (New York: Columbia Business School Publishing, 2014).

245. Goetzmann, *Money Changes Everything*, p. 317.

246. Goetzmann, *Money Changes Everything*, pp. 398–99.

247. Karl Marx, *Capital, A Critique of Political Economy*, Vol. 1, *Book One: The Process of Production of Capital* (Moscow: Progress Publishers, 1867), p. 533. Broad-based secondary-market trading of bonds was integral to the financial sector that developed in medieval Venice. Goetzmann, *Money Changes Everything*, pp. 221–37.

248. Marx, *Capital*, p. 533.

249. Marx, *Capital*, pp. 533–34.

250. There was, of course, a great deal of debate over this proposition. According to economists M. C. Howard and J. E. King, some believed that the Great Depression indicated that "capitalism was doomed, either to protracted stagnation or to imminent economic breakdown." Howard and King, "Marxian Economics and the Great Depression," in *A History of Marxian Economics, Radical Economics* (London: Palgrave, 1992), p. 4.

251. John Maynard Keynes, *The General Theory of Employment, Interest and Money*, Vol. 2 (New York: Cambridge University Press, 2013), p. 159.

252. Keynes, *Employment, Interest and Money*, p. 153. He argued that as ownership became more widely dispersed in the population, "the element of real knowledge in the valuation of investments ... seriously declined."

253. In fact, essentially the same critique could have been leveled at financial markets in, for example, ancient Greece. Goetzmann, *Money Changes Everything*, pp. 73–102.

254. Larry Elliot, "John Maynard Keynes: 'A Great Economist but Poor Currency Trader,'" *The Guardian*, January 12, 2006.

255. Keynes, *Employment, Interest and Money*, p. 159.

256. Keynes, *Employment, Interest and Money*, p. 160.

257. This arbitrary distinction is also reminiscent of the "real bills doctrine," the now-discredited theory that held that banks would lend the "right" quantity of money provided their loans were tied to real output. Some of the earliest directors of the Federal Reserve created economic disturbances because they adhered to this flawed doctrine. See Thomas M. Humphrey and Richard H. Timberlake, *Gold, the Real Bills Doctrine, and the Fed: Sources of Monetary Disorder, 1922–1938* (Washington: Cato Institute, 2019).

258. James Tobin, "On the Efficiency of the Financial System" (Fred Hirsch Memorial Lecture, New York, May 15, 1984), p. 8.

259. In the 1970s, Tobin popularized a ratio now known as Tobin's q, but this ratio is merely a market-value-to-replacement-value concept, one that does not estimate the fundamental long-run value of an asset. Stephen Ross, Randolph

Westerfield, and Jeffrey Jaffe, *Corporate Finance*, 5th ed. (Boston: Irwin/McGraw-Hill, 1999), pp. 37–38.

260. Tobin, "On the Efficiency of the Financial System," p. 10. Tobin argued that derivatives contained "redundancy," and that the "new options and futures contracts … serve mainly to allow greater leverage to short-term speculators and arbitrageurs."

261. Tobin, "On the Efficiency of the Financial System," p. 11.

262. Anthony Bianco, "The Casino Society: Playing with Fire," *Business Week*, September 16, 1985. This article was widely cited during the 1980s, including in *The Atlantic*, the *New York Times*, and the socialist magazine *Monthly Review*, as well as in speeches by SEC commissioners and the SEC general counsel.

263. Beginning in the 1990s, academic critics of financial markets have increasingly used the term "financialization" to characterize "the vastly expanded role of finance in contemporary politics, economy and society." Philip Mader, Daniel Mertens, and Natascha van der Zwan, "Financialization: An Introduction," in the *Routledge International Handbook of Financialization*, ed. Mader, Mertens, and van der Zwan (New York: Routledge, 2021), pp. 1–16. Although the origin of the term remains obscure, John Bellamy Foster, the editor of the socialist magazine *Monthly Review*, credits the use of the term to Kevin Phillips, the author of the 1993 book *Boiling Point*." Foster, "The Financialization of Capitalism," *Monthly Review*, April 1, 2007; Phillips, *Boiling Point* (New York: Random House, 1993).

264. Bianco, "The Casino Society."

265. Tobin, "On the Efficiency of the Financial System," p. 4 (emphasis added). Tobin claimed that there were too many shares of stock, that they were overvalued, and that the average holding period was too low, but he made no reference at all to what might be the appropriate volume, value, or holding period.

266. This statement is meant only in a general sense. Plotting multiple countries through time, for instance, results in no particularly strong pattern that supports any conclusions regarding this ratio.

267. That number is from 2023, when the US population stood at more than 330 million. New York Stock Exchange, "Daily US Equity Matched Volumes," Intercontinental Exchange Inc., 2023. These kinds of statistics demonstrate that both the US economy and its capital markets have grown, but they say nothing about whether any of that growth was harmful in some way, or whether financial market activity exceeded an optimal level.

268. Real GDP in 1947 was $2.176 trillion, versus $8.668 trillion in 1985. It is currently 10 times its size in 1947, with GDP of $22.49 trillion in 2023. US Bureau of Economic Analysis, "Real Gross Domestic Product," retrieved from FRED, Federal Reserve Bank of St. Louis, January 5, 2024.

269. Norbert Michel and Jai Kedia, "American Compass Dystopia: The 'Decline' in Investment," *Cato at Liberty* (blog), July 19, 2023.

270. Michel and Kedia, "American Compass Dystopia."

271. American Compass, *Rebuilding American Capitalism: A Handbook for Conservative Policymakers* (Washington: American Compass, 2023), p. 58. Also see pp. 55–56.

272. The increased use of debt can be seen in banking industry trends. For instance, in real terms (inflation adjusted to 2022 using the Consumer Price Index), US banks reported total assets of $388 billion in 1900, and $1 trillion in 1934, at the middle of the Great Depression. As of 2022, US banks reported total assets of $22.3 trillion. United States Comptroller of the Currency, *The Banking Structure in Evolution: A Response to Public Demand*, 102nd Annual Report (Washington, Government Printing Office, 1964), p. 7; Federal Deposit Insurance Corporation, BankFind Suite: Find Annual Historical Bank Data.

273. Thomas Franck, "Elizabeth Warren Rips Stock Buybacks as 'Nothing but Paper Manipulation,'" CNBC, March 2, 2021.

274. Senator Tammy Baldwin, "U.S. Senator Tammy Baldwin Reintroduces Legislation to Rein in Stock Buybacks and Give Workers a Voice on Corporate Boards," news release, March 27, 2019. In 2019, Rep. Jesús "Chuy" García (D-IL) introduced the Reward Work Act, which would ban companies from purchasing their own securities on a national exchange. In 2023, Garcia reintroduced the bill, with Reps. Ro Khanna (D-CA) and Val Hoyle (D-OR) as co-sponsors. "Representatives García, Hoyle, and Khanna Reintroduce Legislation to Ban Stock Buybacks," news release, May 25, 2023.

275. Ylan Mui, "GOP Sen Marco Rubio Takes Aim at Stock Buybacks, an Issue under Attack by Democrats," CNBC, February 12, 2019.

276. Aya Benlakhder et al., "Prime Numbers: Share Repurchases Still Don't Prop Up Value," McKinsey & Company, April 11, 2023. Even some of the staunchest academic critics of share repurchases fail to provide evidence that the repurchases crowd out value-creating capabilities. They also all but ignore that a repurchase is an exchange of cash for shares—the recipient of the cash is no longer a shareholder. William Lazonick, "Profits without Prosperity," *Harvard Business Review*, September 2014.

277. Companies may also repurchase shares to change the company's capital structure, effect tax strategies, or signal views about the company's stock price. Michael C. Jensen, "Agency Cost of Free Cash Flow, Corporate Finance, and Takeovers," *American Economic Review* 76, no. 2 (May 1986); Paul Asquith and David W. Mullins Jr., "Signaling with Dividends, Stock Repurchases, and Equity Issues," *Financial Management* 15, no. 3 (1986): 27–44; Amy K. Dittmar, "Why Do Firms Repurchase Stock," *Journal of Business* 73, no. 3 (2000): 331–35.

278. Merton Miller, "Financial Markets and Economic Growth," *Journal of Applied Corporate Finance* 11, no. 3 (1998): 14.

279. Miller, "Financial Markets and Economic Growth," p. 14.

Box 4.1

a. It is also incorrect to view the broader private equity industry as a recent invention. Its roots date to, at least, the 1850s. Marc Moore, "Private Equity's Neglected Pre-History: A Trans-Atlantic Perspective," Faculty of Laws University College London Law Research Paper No. 09/2024, March 2024, https://papers.ssrn.com/sol3/papers.cfm?abstract_id=4774618; Vincent Carosso, *Investment Banking in America*, (Cambridge: Harvard University Press, 1970), pp. 27–28.

b. Gheorghe Hurduzeu and Maria-Floriana Popescu, "The History of Junk Bonds and Leveraged Buyouts," *Procedia Economics and Finance* 32, no. 4 (2015): 1270; John Steele Gordon, "Andrew Carnegie and the Creation of U.S. Steel," Bill of Rights Institute, n.d.

c. Daniel Dematos, "Ford's 1919 Management Buyout," *The Tontine Coffee House* (blog), May 10, 2021.

d. Dematos, "Ford's 1919 Management Buyout."

e. Ulf Axelson et al., "Borrow Cheap, Buy High? The Determinants of Leverage and Pricing in Buyouts," National Bureau of Economic Research Working Paper no. 15952, April 2010.

f. Steven N. Kaplan and Per Strömberg, "Leveraged Buyouts and Private Equity," *Journal of Economic Perspectives* 23, no. 1 (2009): 129. For general information on LBOs, see W. Carl Kester and Timothy A. Luehrman, "Rehabilitating the Leveraged Buyout," *Harvard Business Review*, May–June 1995; and Kennedy Chinyamutangira, "Private Equity Deal Activity Remains Resilient Despite Leveraged Loan Market," *Real Economy Blog*, January 19, 2023.

g. Edith S. Hotchkiss, David C. Smith, and Per Strömberg, "Private Equity and the Resolution of Financial Distress," *Review of Corporate Finance Studies* no. 4 (2021): 694–747. The research also shows that there was no clear upward trend in debt default during the period before 2006 among private-equity-backed firms, and in 2008 the non-private-equity-backed firms had the highest default frequencies.

Box 4.2

a. For decades, the accepted empirical evidence has been that any negative relationship between share repurchases and investment is driven by a lack in investment opportunities. See, for example, Gustavo Grullon and Roni Michaely, "The Information Content of Share Repurchase Programs," *Journal of Finance* 59, no. 2 (2004): 651–80.

b. Mark J. Roe, "Looking for the Economy-Wide Effects of Stock Market Short-Termism," Harvard Law School, December 14, 2021, pp. 6–7; Norbert Michel and Jai Kedia, "American Compass Dystopia: The 'Decline' in Investment," *Cato at Liberty* (blog), July 19, 2023.

c. Securities and Exchange Commission, "Response to Congress: Negative Net Equity Issuance," December 23, 2020, p. 14.

d. Securities and Exchange Commission, "Response to Congress."

e. Securities and Exchange Commission, "Response to Congress."

f. American Compass, "Back to Basics for Corporate Finance: Ban Stock Buybacks and Repeal Business Interest Deductibility," American Compass Policy Brief no. 22, May 25, 2023.

g. Securities and Exchange Commission, "Purchases of Certain Equity Securities by the Issuer and Others; Adoption of Safe Harbor," Final Rule, 47 Fed. Reg., 53,333 (November 26, 1982).

h. Securities and Exchange Commission, "Division of Trading and Markets: Answers to Frequently Asked Questions Concerning Rule 10b-18 ('Safe Harbor' for Issuer Repurchases)," December 2, 2016; Stanislav Dolgopolov, "Insider Trading," Econlib, 2023.

i. Jennifer J. Schulp, comment letter on "Share Repurchase Disclosure Modernization," April 1, 2022. This acknowledgment by the SEC featured prominently in the Fifth Circuit Court of Appeals' decision to vacate a 2023 SEC rulemaking on stock buybacks. In that case, the Fifth Circuit found that the SEC failed to consider comments made relating to the "prevalence of improperly motivated buybacks— the very concern motivating the SEC's [ ] rulemaking." *Chamber of Commerce of the USA v. SEC*, 85 F.4th 760, 776 (5th Cir. 2023) at 19. According to the Court, "If opportunistic or improperly motivated buybacks are not genuine problems, then there is no rational basis for investors to experience any of the uncertainty the SEC now claims warrants the rule." *Chamber of Commerce v. SEC*, 85 F.4th at 777.

j. The 1982 final rule explains that share repurchases had been the subject of several previous rule proposals, dating back as far as 1967. Securities and Exchange Commission, "Purchases of Certain Equity Securities by the Issuer and Others." Separately, evidence suggests that "the proportion of companies that repurchased shares increased from less than 27% in 1972 to more than 84% in 2000." Alvin Chen and Olga A. Obizhaeva, *Stock Buyback Motivations and Consequences: A Literature Review*, (Charlottesville, VA: CFA Institute Research Foundation, 2022), p. 7.

k. Harold Bierman Jr. and Richard West, "The Acquisition of Common Stock by the Corporate Issuer," *Journal of Finance.* 21, no. 4 (1966): 687–96.

Box 4.3

a. Anthony Bianco, "The Casino Society: Playing with Fire," *Business Week,* September 16, 1985.

b. For information on derivatives' use in the 1990s, as the markets continued to grow, see Knowledge at Wharton Staff, "How Companies Use Derivatives," April 8, 1999; and Gordon M. Bodnar, and Gunther Gebhardt, "Derivatives Usage in Risk Management by US and German Non-Financial Firms: A Comparative Study," *Journal of International Financial Management and Accounting* 10, no. 3 (1999): 153–87.

CHAPTER 5

280. Mark Flannery, "Supervising Bank Safety and Soundness: Some Open Issues," Federal Reserve Bank of San Francisco, Conference on Safe and Sound Banking: Past, Present, and Future, August 17–18, 2006.

281. For an introductory overview, see Michael P. Malloy and William A. Lovett, *Banking and Financial Institutions Law*, 9th edition, West Academic, St. Paul: Minnesota, 2019; and Karol K. Sparks, *The Keys to Banking Law: A Handbook for Lawyers*, 3rd edition (Chicago: American Bar Association, 2020).

282. Julie Anderson Hill, "When Bank Examiners Get It Wrong: Financial Institution Appeals of Material Supervisory Determinations," University of Alabama Legal Studies Research Paper no. 2494634, September 10, 2014 (accessed March 10, 2016).

283. The OCC is an independent bureau of the US Department of the Treasury, and FinCEN is a bureau of the US Department of the Treasury. In addition to the OCC and FinCEN, the Internal Revenue Service imposes a wide variety of information-reporting and due-diligence requirements on financial institutions. Additionally, if a bank sells investments to customers, its broker-dealer affiliate is subject to regulation by the Financial Industry Regulatory Authority.

284. Uniform Commercial Code, accessed March 21, 2016. The UCC is not actually "uniform" throughout the country. Different states have enacted somewhat different versions.

285. The US banking system has always consisted of significant state involvement and regulation. Howard Bodenhorn, *State Banking in Early America: A New Economic History* (New York: Oxford University Press, 2003).

286. FDIC Improvement Act, 12 US Code § 1831a.

287. All federally chartered banks, and all Federal Reserve member banks, are required to have FDIC deposit insurance. All other banks (state-chartered, non-Fed-member banks) are subject to their state's requirements, and most states now require FDIC deposit insurance as a condition of operating a bank.

288. Title VI of Dodd-Frank, Pub. L. 111–203, July 21, 2010, broadened the Fed's holding company authority. See "Title VI: New Authority for the Fed," in *Dodd-Frank: What It Does and Why It's Flawed*, ed. Hester Peirce and James Broughel (Arlington, VA: Mercatus Center at George Mason University, 2012), pp. 66–75. Additionally, all bank holding companies are subject to state regulations.

289. Pub. L. 81–797, 12 US Code §§ 1811 *et seq.*; 12 US Code § 1813(q); 12 US Code § 1828(c)(2).

290. This section ignores the bank resolution process conducted by the FDIC, as well as the federal government's decision to provide a systemic risk exception, thus allowing the FDIC to cover uninsured depositors. See Norbert Michel, "SVB Debacle Brings the Fed One Step Closer to Becoming Provider of First Resort,"

Forbes, March 23, 2023; and, Norbert Michel, "McKernan Underscores Problems with FDIC's Systemic Risk Exception," *Forbes*, May 16, 2023.

291. 12 US Code § 1820(d)(1).

292. Federal Deposit Insurance Corporation, "Uniform Financial Institutions Rating System," Notice of Adoption of Policy Statement, 62 Fed. Reg., 752 (January 6, 1997). This system was adopted in 1979 by the Federal Financial Institutions Examination Council (FFIEC), an interagency regulatory body that consists of the Federal Reserve Board of Governors, the FDIC, the National Credit Union Administration, the OCC, and the Consumer Financial Protection Bureau. The FFIEC is empowered to prescribe uniform principles, standards, and report forms for federal regulators, with the goal of promoting "consistency in such examination and to insure progressive and vigilant supervision." See Title X of the Financial Institutions Regulatory and Interest Rate Control Act of 1978, 12 US Code § 3301.

293. Sensitivity to market risk (the S) was added in 1996. Federal Reserve Board of Governors, "Uniform Financial Institutions Rating System," news release, December 24, 1996.

294. Banks receive not only a rating for each CAMELS component, but also a composite CAMELS rating. The composite rating is not an average. Instead, the composite rating reflects the "examiners' informed judgment as to how the individual components ratings are combined to provide a summary measure of a bank's overall condition." Lewis Gaul and Jonathan Jones, "CAMELS Ratings and Their Information Content," Office of the Comptroller of the Currency, 2021, p. 5.

295. Federal Deposit Insurance Corporation, "Uniform Financial Institutions Rating System," p. 752.

296. The bank has to be in "generally sound financial condition" (12 C.F.R. § 201.4) and generally have a composite CAMELS rating of 1, 2, or 3. Board of Governors of the Federal Reserve System, "Interagency Advisory on the Use of the Federal Reserve's Primary Credit Program in Effective Liquidity Management," news release, January 9, 2003, p. 2. According to the Fed's guidance, "Under very limited circumstances, the Federal Reserve may consider proposals from organizations with one or more component ratings of '3' or a composite rating of '3' for safety and soundness." Board of Governors of the Federal Reserve System, Supervision and Regulation Letters, "SR 14-2/CA 14-1: Enhancing Transparency in the Federal Reserve's Applications Process," February 24, 2014.

297. 12 C.F.R. § 327.16.

298. 12 US Code § 1843(l); 12 US Code § 1841(o)(9).

299. For restrictions on brokered deposits, see 12 US Code § 1831f(a); for restrictions on asset-size growth, see 12 US Code § 1831o(e)(3); for restrictions on branching and acquiring new lines of business or other financial firms, see 12 US Code § 1831o(e) (4); for restrictions on appointing new officers and directors, see 12 C.F.R. § 5.51.

300. 12 US Code § 3907; 12 US Code § 1831o(c).

301. 12 US Code § 3907(a)(1).

302. 12 US Code § 3907(a)(2).

303. The Basel III standards are a set of measures developed by the Basel Committee on Banking Supervision in response to the financial crisis of 2007–2009. See Bank for International Settlements, "Basel III: International Regulatory Framework for Banks," accessed April 21, 2021.

304. 12 C.F.R. § 217.1(d)(3).

305. 12 C.F.R. § 225.8; 12 C.F.R. § 217.1. For FDIC-regulated institutions, risk-weighted capital rules are also based on Basel III. 12 C.F.R. § 324.10; 12 C.F.R. § 325.103.

306. 12 US Code § 3907(b)(1); 12 US Code § 1818.

307. Julie Anderson Hill, "Regulating Bank Reputation Risk," *Georgia Law Review* 54 (2020): 543–53.

308. Hill, "Regulating Bank Reputation Risk," pp. 532, 545.

309. Office of the Comptroller of the Currency, *Comptroller's Handbook: Examination Process, Large Bank Supervision* (Washington: OCC, 2018), p. 64. The National Credit Union Administration has a similar definition to the OCC's; see Hill, "Regulating Bank Reputation Risk," p. 546.

310. Office of the Comptroller of the Currency, *Comptroller's Handbook*, p. 30.

311. Office of the Comptroller of the Currency, *Comptroller's Handbook*, p. 31.

312. Board of Governors of the Federal Reserve, Supervision and Regulation letter 95-51 (SUP), November 14, 1995, revised February 26, 2021 (emphasis added).

313. Federal Deposit Insurance Corporation, "Basic Examination Concepts and Guidelines," in *Risk Management Manual of Examination Policies* (Washington: FDIC, 2021), p. 25.

314. Hill, "Regulating Bank Reputation Risk," p. 532. As discussed in chapter 7, the FDIC's interactions with payday lenders gained widespread notoriety in 2013 through Operation Choke Point, a Department of Justice–led multiagency initiative that, ostensibly, was "intended to protect consumers from fraud perpetrated by fraudulent merchants, financial institutions, and financial intermediaries known as third-party payment processors (TPPP)." Federal Deposit Insurance Corporation, Office of the Inspector General, "The FDIC's Role in Operation Choke Point and Supervisory Approach to Institutions That Conducted Business with Merchants Associated with High-Risk Activities," OIG Report no. AUD-15-008, September 2015, p. 1.

315. 12 US Code § 1818(a)(2)(A)(i).

316. 12 US Code § 1818(b)(7).

317. 12 US Code § 1818(b).

318. 12 C.F.R. 32.5 provides regulations for combinations of borrowers.

319. 12 US Code § 84(a)(1). Also see 12 C.F.R. 32.3. This requirement also applies to national savings associations.

320. 12 US Code § 84(a)(2).

321. 12 US Code § 84(d)(1) (emphasis added).

322. 12 US Code § 5365(a)(1).

323. Nationwide branch banking and government-backed deposit insurance were two competing reform proposals that predate the creation of the Federal Reserve in 1913, whereas support for deposit insurance dates as far back as the early 19th century. Although the abysmal record of state-backed deposit insurance funds seemed to sound the death knell of a federal deposit scheme, nearly 4,000 banks failed in 1933, making it much easier for Congress to create the FDIC. And although the creation of the FDIC in 1933 could have marked the end of the push to expand nationwide bank branching, Congress made interstate branch banking fully legal in 1994 when it passed the Riegle-Neal Interstate Banking and Branching Efficiency Act. Charles W. Calomiris and Stephen H. Haber, *Fragile by Design: The Political Origins of Banking Crises and Scarce Credit* (Princeton, NJ: Princeton University Press, 2014), p. 191; Federal Deposit Insurance Corporation, *Managing the Crisis: The FDIC and RTC Experience—Chronological Overview* (Washington: FDIC, 2018); Bill Medley, "Riegle-Neal Interstate Banking and Branching Efficiency Act of 1994," Federal Reserve History, September 1994.

324. Pub. L. 89-695, 80 Stat. 1028. The main sections of the law (Titles I and II) were set to expire on June 30, 1972, but Section 908 of the Housing and Urban Development Act of 1970 repealed that expiration.

325. Financial Institutions Supervisory Act of 1966, hearings before the United States House of Representatives, Committee on Banking and Currency, 89th Cong., 2nd sess., September 15, 1966, pp. 27-33.

326. Between 1980 and 1994, approximately 1,300 savings and loans failed (32 percent of the total in 1980). These failures decimated the Federal Home Loan Bank System, but Congress decided to keep that system afloat by expanding membership to commercial banks. Section 704 of the FIRREA allowed any insured depository institution to join the Federal Home Loan Bank System provided it held at least 10 percent of its total assets in residential mortgages. Currently, 6,500 financial institutions are in the Federal Home Loan Bank System. Federal Deposit Insurance Corporation, "The Banking Crises of the 1980s and Early 1990s: Summary and Implications," in *History of the Eighties: Lessons for the* Future, vol. 1, *An Examination of the Banking Crises of the 1980s and Early 1990s* (Washington: FDIC, 2023), pp. 3–86; FHLBanks, "Facts at a Glance," 2023.

327. 12 US Code § 1831o.

328. For an overview, see Noelle Richards, "Federal Deposit Insurance Corporation Improvement Act of 1991," Federal Reserve History, December 19, 1991.

329. TILA: Pub. L. 90–321, 15 US Code §§ 1601 *et seq.*, as amended, and 12 C.F.R. Part 226——Truth in Lending (Regulation Z). FCRA: Pub. L. 91-508, 84 Stat. 1127-46, 15 US Code §§ 1681, *et seq.* BSA: Pub. L. 91–508 § 231, 84 Stat. 1122; Norbert Michel and Jennifer Schulp, "Revising the Bank Secrecy Act to Protect Privacy and Deter Criminals," Cato Institute Policy Analysis no. 932, July 26, 2022. ECOA: Pub. L. 94–239, 90 Stat. 251, 15 US Code §§ 1691, *et seq.* RESPA: Pub. L. 93–533, 12 US Code §§ 2601 *et seq.*, as amended. CRA: Pub. L. 95-128, 91 Stat. 1147 (Title VIII of the Housing and Community Development Act of 1977), 12 US Code §§ 2901, *et seq.* Act of 1980: Pub. L. 96-221, 94 Stat. 132; The Banking Acts of 1933 (the Glass-Steagall Act) and of 1935, respectively, outlawed interest payments on demand deposits and gave the Fed the authority to set interest-rate ceilings on time and savings deposits for member and nonmember banks. R. Alton Gilbert, "Requiem for Regulation Q: What It Did and Why It Passed Away," Federal Reserve Bank of St. Louis, February 1986, pp. 22–37; Regulators and at least some members of Congress also believed that Regulation Q could be used to prevent interest rates from rising, a belief that proved to be incorrect. See Gilbert, "Requiem for Regulation Q"; Kenneth J. Robinson, "Depository Institutions Deregulation and Monetary Control Act of 1980," Federal Reserve History, March 1980. Act of 1983: Pub. L. 98-181, 97 Stat. 1278. The act was Title IX of the Department of Housing and Urban Development Independent Agencies Appropriation Act of 1984. Before this law, federal banking regulators made "their subjective evaluations of capital adequacy based on a combination of capital ratios and their evaluation of other important factors affecting safety and soundness, such as the quality of assets, the effectiveness of management, and current and prospective earnings." Roger Tufts and Paul Moloney, "The History of Supervisory Expectations for Capital Adequacy: Part II (1984–2021)," Moments in History, Office of the Comptroller of the Currency, October 25, 2022. Act of 1994: Pub. L. 103-328, 108 Stat. 2338; Pub. L. 106-102, 113 Stat. 1338. GLBA: Dafna Avraham, Patricia Selvaggi, and James Vickery, "A Structural View of U.S. Bank Holding Companies," Federal Reserve Bank of New York *Economic Policy Review*, July 2012, p. 67. Act of 2010: Pub. L.111-203, 124 Stat. 1376. Act of 2010; This authority is commonly referred to as the power to designate firms as "systemically important financial institutions," but the law does not actually identify the firms as such. 12 US Code § 5323(a)(1). Norbert Michel, ed., *The Case against Dodd-Frank: How the "Consumer Protection" Law Endangers Americans* (Washington: Heritage Foundation, 2016); Michel, *The Case against Dodd-Frank.*

330. For a longer list, see Federal Deposit Insurance Corporation, "Chronology of Selected Banking Laws," last updated November 16, 2021.

331. See Code of Federal Regulations, "Title 12, Banks and Banking."

332. For additional description, see Nicholas L. Georgeakopoulos, *The Logic of Securities Law* (Cambridge and New York: Cambridge University Press, 2017), pp. 25–28.

333. SEC Commissioner Hester Peirce describes it well: "Even though Congress did not set the SEC up to be a merit regulator, the securities laws are not hands-off the markets either." She then goes on to describe the ways in which the SEC's regulatory approach "has turned increasingly prescriptive" in recent years. Peirce, "Pourquoi Pas? Securities Regulation and the American Dream" (speech, Association of Private Enterprise Education, Washington, April 8, 2024).

334. 15 US Code § 78o(c)(3); 17 C.F.R. § 240.15c3-1. This rule is very different from a bank's capital rules, largely because a bank is very different from a broker-dealer. See Erik Sirri, "Securities Markets and Regulatory Reform" (speech, National Economists Club, Washington, April 9, 2009).

335. See 17 C.F.R. 240.15c3-1 for the current rule. For a history of the rule's development, see Nicholas Wolfson and Egon Guttman, "The Net Capital Rules for Brokers and Dealers," *Stanford Law Review* 24, no. 4 (1972): 603–43.

336. It is also the case that "very similar financial products may receive very different regulatory treatment based on the institutional label, even when their function is very similar." James J. Angel, "On the Regulation of Investment Advisory Services: Where Do We Go from Here?," Center for Financial Markets and Policy, Georgetown University McDonough School of Business, October 31, 2011, p. 13.

337. This is not a comprehensive review of all the disclosure obligations of a public company. Public companies must also file disclosures relating to their shareholder meetings, about ownership and trading of their shares by company insiders, and about foreign investment by the company, among other things.

338. For more detail on requirements of exemptions from registration, see "Overview of Capital-Raising Exemptions," Securities and Exchange Commission, last modified April 6, 2023.

339. *TSC Industries, Inc. v. Northway, Inc.*, 426 U.S. 438, 449 (1976).

340. Securities and Exchange Commission, "Disclosing the Use of Conflict Minerals," fact sheet, March 14, 2017.

341. Michael Ewens, Kairong Xiao, and Ting Xu, "Regulatory Costs of Being Public: Evidence from Bunching Estimation," *Journal of Financial Economics* 153 (2024): 141–53; Gabriele Lattanzio, William L. Legginson, and Ali Sanati, "Dissecting the Listing Gap: Mergers, Private Equity, or Deregulation," *Journal of Financial Markets* 65, no. 5 (2023): 100836.

342. In addition to the regulatory scheme, the federal securities laws also create private causes of action under which nongovernment plaintiffs can bring suit to recover damages for rule violations. Not every rule can be enforced by a private cause of action—and the scope of available private causes of action has expanded over time. A. C. Pritchard and Robert B. Thompson, *A History of Securities Law in the Supreme Court* (New York: Oxford University Press, 2023), pp. 168–221. This liability scheme—particularly regarding issuers but to a lesser degree to all

regulated market participants—serves an important role in regulating the conduct of market participants.

343. For a detailed discussion of how this system differs from the original statutory framework, see Alexander I. Platt, "The Administrative Origins of Mandatory Disclosure," *Journal of Corporation Law* (forthcoming).

344. Broker-dealer registration is a complicated process in and of itself. See, for example, Securities and Exchange Commission, Division of Trading and Markets, Investor Publications, *Guide to Broker-Dealer Registration* (Washington: SEC, 2008).

345. Securities and Exchange Commission, "Regulation Best Interest: The Broker-Dealer Standard of Conduct," Exchange Act Release no. 86031, 84 FR 33318 (June 5, 2019).

346. The Securities Investor Protection Act of 1970 created the Securities Investor Protection Corporation (SIPC), which oversees the liquidation of member firms that close when the firm is bankrupt or in financial trouble and customer assets are missing. SIPC is a nonprofit membership corporation that expedites the return of customer property by protecting each customer for securities and cash up to $500,000. 15 U.S.C. § 78ccc. SIPC, however, is not a securities equivalent of the FDIC and has no federal taxpayer backing.

347. Mary Jo White, chair, Securities and Exchange Commission, Testimony on "Mitigating Systemic Risk in the Financial Markets through Wall Street Reforms," before the Senate Committee on Banking, Housing, and Urban Affairs, 113th Cong., 1st sess., July 30, 2013. SEC Chair Gary Gensler recently stated, "At the SEC, we are always monitoring markets for systemic risk." Joe Mathiew and Kailey Leinz, "SEC's Gensler: We Do Monitor Systemic Risk," Bloomberg, March 6, 2024.

348. Both the SEC and FINRA have been accused of abusing that discretion by "regulating by enforcement," which refers to using enforcement actions to create new standards and rules, rather than promulgating rules through regular processes. Mark Schoeff Jr., "Finra Engages in Rulemaking by Enforcement: Financial Industry Groups," *Investment News*, June 21, 2017; Peter Chen and A. Valerie Mirko, "Recommendations to the SEC to Modify Its Procedural Framework to Prevent Regulation by Enforcement," white paper, Financial Services Institute, January 2024.

349. Investment Advisers Act of 1940, § 202(a)(11), 15 US Code § 80b-2(11).

350. Investment Advisers Act of 1940, § 203A, 15 US Code § 80b-3a.

351. Securities and Exchange Commission, Amendments to Form ADV, Investment Advisers Act Release no. 2711, March 3, 2008.

352. *SEC v. Capital Gains Research Bureau, Inc.*, 365 U.S. 180, 190–92 (1963).

353. See Robert E. Plaze, "Regulation of Investment Advisers by the U.S. Securities and Exchange Commission," white paper, Proskauer Rose LLP,

June 2018, for a more thorough treatment of investment adviser regulation. The SEC recently adopted new rules applicable to private fund advisers that apply additional requirements and prohibitions. Securities and Exchange Commission, "Private Fund Advisers; Documentation of Registered Adviser Compliance Reviews," Release no. IA-6383, 88 FR 63206, September 14, 2023.

354. Securities and Exchange Commission, "SEC Adopts Amendments to Enhance Private Fund Reporting," Press Release no. 2024-17, February 8, 2024.

355. Securities and Exchange Commission, Division of Examinations, "Investment Advisers: Assessing Risks, Scoping Examinations, and Requesting Documents," Risk Alert, September 6, 2023, p. 1, fn 1. Although broker-dealer exams also use a risk-based component to determining which firms will be examined, FINRA examinations are generally subject to a more regular schedule than investment adviser examinations conducted by the SEC.

356. Securities and Exchange Commission, Division of Examinations, "Investment Advisers: Assessing Risks, Scoping Examinations, and Requesting Documents," Risk Alert, September 6, 2023, p. 1, fn 1.

357. For a more in-depth discussion of investment company regulation, see Investment Company Institute, *How US-Registered Investment Companies Operate and the Core Principles Underlying Their Regulation* (Washington: Investment Company Institute, 2022).

358. The SEC chair Mary Jo White described asset management regulation as "a significant segment of our financial system—and, as we all know, the nature of financial means that changes to *any* significant segment ha[ve] consequences for the others (emphasis in original)." White, "Enhancing Risk Monitoring and Regulatory Safeguards for the Asset Management Industry" (speech, *New York Times* DealBook Opportunities for Tomorrow Conference, New York City, December 11, 2014).

359. Pete Schroeder, "U.S. Regulators Agree to Ramp Up Oversight of Systemically Risky Non-Banks," Reuters, November 3, 2023.

360. According to the SEC, examinations of registered investment companies are prioritized "due to their importance to retail investors, particularly those saving for retirement." Securities and Exchange Commission, Division of Examinations, *2024 Examination Priorities* (Washington: SEC, 2024), p. 15.

361. For a timeline describing regulatory milestones before the establishment of the CFTC, see Commodity Futures Trading Commission, "US Futures Trading and Regulation before the Creation of the CFTC," History of the CFTC, accessed March 4, 2024.

362. The CFTC allows the listing of new contracts under certain circumstance by "self-certification," a process whereby the designated contract market may self-certify that the contract listed complies with the law. In that case, no formal CFTC approval is required to list the contract, but the CFTC can object

to the self-certification. "Listing products for trading by certification," 17 C.F.R. § 40.2 (2011).

363. For example, see Commodity Exchange Act, 7 US Code § 7a-2(c), "Review of event contracts based upon certain excluded commodities," 17 C.F.R. § 40.11 (2011); and Brian D. Quintenz, "Any Given Sunday in the Futures Market," Statement on ErisX RSBIX NFL Contracts and Certain Event Contracts," March 25, 2021.

364. 15 US Code §§ 8302, et seq.; 7 US Code §6a(a)(1).

365. Although the OTC swaps market was not subject to CFTC regulation before the Dodd-Frank Act, most of these derivatives were regulated by banking regulators because banks were the primary users of such instruments. For more on derivatives regulation, see Norbert Michel, "Fixing the Dodd-Frank Derivatives Mess: Repeal Titles VII and VIII," Heritage Foundation Backgrounder no. 3076, November 16, 2015.

366. Securities Act: Pub. L. 73-22, 48 Stat. 74. Securities Exchange Act: Pub. L. 73-291, 48 Stat. 88. Commodity Exchange Act: For a history of pre-CEA legislation, see Commodity Futures Trading Commission, "US Futures Trading and Regulation before the Creation of the CFTC," History of the CFTC, accessed March 4, 2024; Pub. L. 74-675, 49 Stat. 1491. Investment Advisers Act: Pub. L. 76-768, 54 Stat. 789. Investment Company Act: Pub. L. 76-768, 54 Stat. 789. Commodity Futures Trading Commission Act: Pub. L. 93-463, 88 Stat. 1389. Securities Act Amendments: Pub. L. 94-29, 89 Stat. 97; Regulation NMS, 17 C.F.R. §§ 242.600 et seq. Futures Trading Practices Act: Pub. L. 102-546, 106 Stat. 3590. Commodity Futures Modernization Act: Pub. L. 106-554, 114 Stat. 2763A-365. Sarbanes-Oxley Act: Pub. L. 107-204, 116 Stat. 745. Dodd-Frank: Norbert Michel, "Fixing the Regulatory Framework for Derivatives," Heritage Foundation Backgrounder no. 3076, September 14, 2016, p. 5; Pub. L.111-203, 124 Stat. 1376.

367. George A. Selgin, "Legal Restrictions, Financial Weakening, and the Lender of Last Resort," *Cato Journal* 9, no. 2 (1989): 429–59. A similar argument is that unrestricted, or laissez faire, banking is inherently unstable, an argument that often focuses on banks during the so-called free banking laws in the antebellum period. Research has demonstrated, however, that these laws did not allow laissez faire banking and, instead, merely allowed "freer" entry into banking while maintaining regulations on banking activities. See Lawrence H. White, "Regulatory Sources of Instability in Banking," *Cato Journal* 5, no. 3 (1986): 891–97.

368. Calomiris and Haber, *Fragile by Design*, p. 5. If banking is inherently unstable, then experience across nations should be relatively similar, but that has not been the case.

369. Michael Bordo, "Some Historical Evidence 1870–1933 on the Impact and International Transmission of Financial Crises," National Bureau of Economic Research Working Paper no. 1606, April 1985.

370. Calomiris and Haber, *Fragile by Design*, pp. 6–7.

371. One of the few comprehensive studies of bank contagion concludes, "However, there is no evidence to support the widely held belief that, even in the absence of deposit insurance, bank contagion is a holocaust that can bring down solvent banks, the financial system, and even the entire macroeconomy in domino fashion." George Kaufman, "Bank Contagion: A Review of the Theory and Evidence," *Journal of Financial Services Research* 8, no. 2 (1994): 143.

372. George Selgin, "Are Banking Crises Free-Market Phenomena?," *Critical Review*, 8, no. 4, 1994: 598. Selgin also provides a broader discussion of historical examples, including during the Great Depression era. For a full discussion of the lack of contagion during the 2008 financial crisis, see Norbert Michel, *Why Shadow Banking Didn't Cause the Financial Crisis, and Why Regulating Contagion Won't Help* (Washington: Cato Institute, 2022).

373. Selgin, "Are Banking Crises Free-Market Phenomena?," p. 605.

374. Michel, *Why Shadow Banking Didn't Cause the Financial Crisis.*

CHAPTER 6

375. Michael Lewis, *The Big Short: Inside the Doomsday Machine* (New York: W. W. Norton and Co., 2010). The book's dust jacket for example, claims, "The real crash, the silent crash, had taken place over the previous year, in bizarre feeder markets where the sun doesn't shine and the SEC doesn't dare, or bother, to tread."

376. The movie did manage to imply that Fed chair Alan Greenspan's loose monetary policy was a major cause of the crisis, but it didn't say a word about President Bill Clinton's National Partners in Homeownership, a public–private program that set an explicit goal of raising the US homeownership rate from 64 percent to 70 percent by 2000. It was specifically designed to work with Fannie Mae's Trillion-Dollar Commitment, a program that earmarked $1 trillion for affordable housing between 1994 and 2000. Norbert Michel, "The Big Short: A Great Movie, Not a Policy Prescription," *Forbes*, August 10, 2016.

377. Nicola Cetorelli and Stavros Peristiani, "The Role of Banks in Asset Securitization," Federal Reserve Bank of New York *Economic Policy Review*, July 2012, p. 58. In some cases—trustee services, for example—a small group of large custodian banks dominate the asset securitization business.

378. Harald Uhlig, "Mortgage-Backed Securities and the Financial Crisis of 2008: A Post Mortem," research brief, Becker Friedman Institute at the University of Chicago, May 1, 2018.

379. Uhlig, "Financial Crisis of 2008: A Post Mortem."

380. Carrick Mollenkamp et al., "How London Created a Snarl in Global Markets," *Wall Street Journal*, October 18, 2007.

381. Had banks been required to record these commitments on their balance sheets, they would have needed additional capital as the securities were issued. Instead, the off-balance-sheet device allowed banks to delay the higher capital charge until, and only if, they experienced future losses. Christian Wolff and Nikolaos Papanikolaou, "The Global Crisis beyond Banks' Balance Sheets," Centre for Economic Policy Research, December 6, 2015.

382. Norbert Michel and John Ligon, "Basel III Capital Standards Do Not Reduce the Too-Big-to-Fail Problem," Heritage Foundation Backgrounder no. 2905, April 23, 2014.

383. Walker F. Todd, "FDICIA's Emergency Liquidity Provisions," Cleveland Federal Reserve *Economic Review*, no. Q III (1993), p. 20. At the very least, this change increased the chances the Fed would see a nonbanking liquidity crisis as one in which it would be obligated to lend.

384. Darryll Hendricks and Beverly Hirtle, "Bank Capital Requirements for Market Risk: The Internal Models Approach," Federal Reserve Bank of New York *Economic Policy Review*, December 1997.

385. Jeffrey Friedman, "A Perfect Storm of Ignorance," *Cato Policy Report*, January–February 2010; Jeffrey Friedman and Wladimir Kraus, "A Silver Lining to the Financial Crisis: A More Realistic View of Capitalism," *Wall Street Journal*, February 22, 2010; Stephen Matteo Miller, "The Recourse Rule, Regulatory Arbitrage, and the Financial Crisis," Mercatus Center Working Paper, August 3, 2017.

386. Congress expanded derivatives priorities in 1982, 1984, 1994, 2005, and 2006 as well. Mark J. Roe, "The Derivatives Market's Payment Priorities as Financial Crisis Accelerator," *Stanford Law Review* 63, no. 3 (2011): 539; Edward R. Morrison and Joerg Riegel, "Financial Contracts and the New Bankruptcy Code: Insulating Markets from Bankrupt Debtors and Bankruptcy Judges," Columbia Law and Economics Working Paper no. 291, January 2006; Thomas M. Hoenig and Charles S. Morris, "Restructuring the Banking System to Improve Safety and Soundness," in *The Social Value of the Financial Sector: Too Big to Fail or Just Too Big*, ed. Viral V. Acharya et al. (Hackensack, NJ: World Scientific, 2013), pp. 401–25.

387. Anthony Bianco, "The Casino Society: Playing with Fire," *Business Week*, September 16, 1985, p. 83.

388. University of Houston, "Reaganomics," Digital History, 2021; Federal Deposit Insurance Corporation, "The Savings and Loan Crisis and Its Relationship to Banking," in *History of the Eighties: Lessons for the Future*, vol. 1, *An Examination of the Banking Crises of the 1980s and Early 1990s* (Washington: FDIC, 1997), p. 177.

389. American Compass, *Rebuilding American Capitalism: A Handbook for Conservative Policymakers* (Washington: American Compass, 2023), p. 29.

390. Joao Rafael Cunha, "The Advent of a New Banking System in the U.S.—Financial Deregulation in the 1980s," St. Andrews University, School of Economics and Finance Discussion Paper no. 2003, April 29, 2020.

391. Laura Litvan and Brian Faler, "Congress Pushes for Bigger Role in Resolving Financial Crisis," Bloomberg, September 16, 2008.

392. "Transcript of Second McCain, Obama Debate," CNN.com, October 7, 2008.

393. "Elizabeth Warren Explains the Effect That Deregulation Has Had on Our Financial System and Economy," *Dan Rather Reports*, 2009, YouTube video.

394. David Super, "Now Is the Time to Guard against Reckless Banking Legislation," *The Hill*, March 20, 2023.

395. Norbert Michel and Tamara Skinner, "The Popular Narrative about Financial Deregulation Is Wrong," *Daily Signal*, July 29, 2016.

396. The total is from updated versions of agency-provided data used in James L. Gattuso, "Red Tape Rising: Regulatory Trends in the Bush Years," Heritage Foundation Backgrounder no. 2116, March 25, 2008. The figure includes regulations promulgated by the Federal Reserve, the SEC, and the Department of the Treasury.

397. These figures are adjusted to constant 2000 dollars. James L. Gattuso, "Meltdowns and Myths: Did Deregulation Cause the Financial Crisis?," Heritage Foundation WebMemo no. 2109, October 22, 2008.

398. Gattuso, "Meltdowns and Myths."

399. Gattuso, "Meltdowns and Myths."

400. Mark Calabria, "Did Deregulation Cause the Financial Crisis?," *Cato Policy Report*, July–August 2009.

401. Although in aggregate the bank regulatory agencies show a slight decline (from 13,310 in 2000 to 12,190 in 2008), the decrease was driven by reductions in staff at the regional Federal Reserve Banks due to cutbacks in their check-clearing activities (which started relying more on electronic processing), and at the FDIC due to reductions in its resolution staff after the artificial increase during the savings and loan crisis.

402. These dollar figures are in constant 2000 dollars. See Veronique de Rugy and Melinda Warren, "The Incredible Growth of the Regulators' Budget," Mercatus Center Working Paper no. 08-36, Mercatus Center at George Mason University, September 2008, pp. 3–4.

403. This list is compiled from popular critiques of specific policy changes that, supposedly, contributed to the 2008 crisis because they deregulated financial markets. Several proponents of the conventional deregulation story provide lists of bills that they claimed deregulated financial markets. See, for example, Matthew Sherman, "A Short History of Financial Deregulation in the United States," Center for Economic and Policy Research, July 2009. For an explanation of various regulatory rulemakings as well as legislation, see Arnold Kling, "Not What They Had in Mind: A History of Policies That Produced the Financial Crisis of 2008," Mercatus Center research paper, Mercatus Center at George Mason University, 2009.

404. See, for example, Kevin Cirilli, "Warren Calls for Return of Glass-Steagall," *The Hill*, July 14, 2015.

405. The commonly used term "Glass–Steagall" refers to four sections of the Banking Act of 1933. Many misconceptions surround the Glass-Steagall Act. For instance, one of the most in-depth studies of the Glass-Steagall Act states, "The evidence from the pre-Glass-Steagall period is totally inconsistent with the belief that banks' securities activities or investments caused them to fail or caused the financial system to collapse." See George Benston, *The Separation of Commercial and Investment Banking* (New York: Oxford University Press, 1990), p. 41. Also see Norbert Michel, "The Glass-Steagall Act: Unraveling the Myth," Heritage Foundation Backgrounder no. 3104, April 28, 2016.

406. The practice of *underwriting* securities refers to assuming the risk that an issue of securities (stocks, for example), will be fully sold to investors; the practice of dealing securities typically refers to holding an inventory of securities to facilitate trades (buying and selling) for customers.

407. GLBA, § 101. A copy of the 1999 act is available at Authenticated US Government Information, S. 900, 106th Congress, 1st sess.

408. Dafna Avraham, Patricia Selvaggi, and James Vickery, "A Structural View of U.S. Bank Holding Companies," *Federal Reserve Bank of New York Economic Policy Review*, July 2012, p. 67.

409 Code of Federal Regulations, Title 12, Ch. II § 225.82.

410. "FDIC Consumer Compliance Examination Manual," Gramm-Leach-Bliley Act, April 2021.

411. Thomas J. McCool, "Federal Home Loan Bank System: An Overview of Changes and Current Issues Affecting the System," GAO-05-489T, US Government Accountability Office, 2005.

412. The Banking Acts of 1933 and 1935, respectively, outlawed interest payments on demand deposits and gave the Fed the authority to set interest-rate ceilings on time and savings deposits for member and nonmember banks. See R. Alton Gilbert, "Requiem for Regulation Q: What It Did and Why It Passed Away," Federal Reserve Bank of St. Louis, February 1986. The DMCA left the prohibition of paying interest on demand deposits in place, though the 2010 Dodd-Frank Act eliminated that ban.

413. Thrift institutions (mutual savings banks and savings and loan institutions) were not subject to the rate ceiling until 1966. See Gilbert, "Requiem for Regulation Q."

414. Gilbert, "Requiem for Regulation Q," p. 30.

415. Gilbert, "Requiem for Regulation Q," p. 30.

416. The Fed administers these rules under Regulation D; see Code of Federal Regulations, Title 12, Chapter II, Subchapter A, Part 204.

417. Richard H. Timberlake Jr., "Legislative Construction of the Monetary Control Act of 1980," *American Economic Review* 75, no. 2, *Papers and Proceedings of the Ninety-Seventh Annual Meeting of the American Economic Association* (1985): 97–102.

418. Jeffrey Rogers Hummel, "The Deregulation and Monetary Control Act of 1980," *Cato Policy Report*, December 1980, p. 5.

419. The DMCA also established nationwide Negotiable Order of Withdrawal, or NOW, accounts and All Savers Certificates, new financial instruments with a floating interest-rate ceiling. Gilbert, "Requiem for Regulation Q," p. 33.

420. Gillian Garcia, "Garn–St Germain Depository Institutions Act of 1982," Federal Reserve History, October 1982; Kenneth J. Robinson, "Savings and Loan Crisis: 1980–1989," Federal Reserve History, November 22, 2013.

421. Gillian Garcia et al., "The Garn–St. Germain Depository Institutions Act of 1982," Federal Reserve Bank of Chicago *Economic Perspectives* 7, no. 2 (1983): 3–31.

422. Arguably, allowing S&Ls to make demand deposits made the regulatory environment more complex because the legal definition of a bank had to be altered to prevent S&Ls from coming under the direct regulatory authority of the Federal Reserve. See Garcia et al., "Garn–St. Germain Depository Institutions Act."

423. Garcia et al., "The Garn–St. Germain Depository Institutions Act," p. 8.

424. For more on the history of federal and state bank regulation, see Christian A. Johnson and Tara Rice, "Assessing a Decade of Interstate Bank Branching," Federal Reserve Bank of Chicago Working Paper no. 2007-3, April 2007.

425. IBBEA, § 101.

426. IBBEA, § 102. Federal Deposit Insurance Act (Pub. L. 81-797; 12 US Code Chapter 16, as amended) defines the appropriate federal banking agency for purposes of which agency regulates which bank (12 US Code § 1813(q)) and determines which federal agency is responsible for approving bank mergers (12 US Code § 1828(c)(2).)

427. 12 US Code § 1831u (b)(2).

428. Arthur Levitt, chair of the US Securities and Exchange Commission, Testimony on S. 2697, Commodity Futures Modernization Act of 2000, before the Senate Committee on Agriculture, Nutrition, and Forestry and Committee on Banking, Housing, and Urban Affairs, 106 Cong., 2nd sess., June 21, 2000.

429. Levitt, Testimony, June 21, 2000.

430. For more on derivatives regulation, see Norbert Michel, "Fixing the Dodd-Frank Derivatives Mess: Repeal Titles VII and VIII," Heritage Foundation Backgrounder no. 3076, November 16, 2015.

431. International Swaps and Derivatives Association, "The Value of Derivatives," 2014.

432. Before 1974, the US Department of Agriculture regulated the futures market, and the first federal statute regulating futures was the Grain Futures Act

of 1922. The Commodity Futures Trading Commission was created in 1974 soon after newspaper reporters blamed a steep increase in food prices on speculative trading. Roberta Romano, "A Thumbnail Sketch of Derivative Securities and Their Regulation," *Maryland Law Review* 55, no. 1 (1996): 1–83.

433. Katerina Simons, "Interest Rate Structure and the Credit Risk of Swaps," Federal Reserve Bank of Boston *New England Economic Review*, July–August 1993, pp. 23–34. Simons also points out, "To the extent that swaps replace on-balance-sheet obligations of counterparties, they reduce rather than increase the credit risk in the financial system" (p. 34).

434. Simons, "Credit Risk of Swaps." p. 34.

435. Office of the Comptroller of the Currency, "Credit Derivatives," OCC Bulletin no. 1996-43, August 12, 1996.

436. Comptroller of the Currency, "OCC's Quarterly Report on Bank Derivatives Activities, Second Quarter 2006," p. 1.

437. Dodd-Frank Title III, 12 US Code, Subchapter III. Also see Board of Governors of the Federal Reserve System, FDIC, OCC, and Office of Thrift Supervision, "Joint Implementation Plan: 301–326 of the Dodd-Frank Wall Street Reform and Consumer Protection Act," 2011.

438. Section 701, Subtitle A (Regulation of the Over-the-Counter Swaps Markets), 15 US Code, Chapter 109, Subchapter I. Furthermore, banking regulators remain responsible (under the new Basel III requirements) for certifying that banks are meeting their regulatory capital ratios, even when they use swaps.

439. See 17 C.F.R. 240.15c3-1 for the current rule. For a history of the rule's development, see Nicholas Wolfson and Egon Guttman, "The Net Capital Rules for Brokers and Dealers," *Stanford Law Review* 24, no. 4 (1972): 603–43.

440. US Government Accountability Office, *Financial Markets Regulation: Financial Crisis Highlights Need to Improve Oversight of Leverage at Financial Institutions and across System*, GAO-09-739 (Washington: GAO, 2009), p. 41; Andrew W. Lo, "Reading about the Financial Crisis: A 21-Book Review," *Journal of Economic Literature* 50, no. 1 (2012): 151–78.

441. "Securities and Exchange Commission: Alternative Net Capital Requirements for Broker-Dealers That Are Part of Consolidated Supervised Entities, Final Rules," 69 Fed. Reg., 34428 (June 21, 2004).

442. "Securities and Exchange Commission: Alternative Net Capital Requirements for Broker-Dealers," p. 34428.

443. Office of Inspector General, "SEC's Oversight of Bear Stearns and Related Entities: The Consolidated Supervised Entity Program," Securities and Exchange Commission Report no. 446-A, September 25, 2008.

444. Erik R. Sirri, "Markets and Regulatory Reform" (speech, National Economists Club, Washington, April 9, 2009). Separately, the SEC inspector general's

report acknowledged that the SEC Division of Trading and Markets was aware of numerous potential red flags before Bear Stearns's collapse "regarding its concentration of mortgage securities, high leverage, shortcomings of risk management in mortgage-backed securities and *lack of compliance* with the spirit of certain Basel II standards, but did not take actions to limit these risk factors" (emphasis added). Office of Inspector General, "SEC's Oversight of Bear Stearns," p. viii.

445. David Beim and Christopher McCurdy, "Federal Reserve Bank of New York Report on Systemic Risk and Bank Supervision," discussion draft, August 18, 2009, p. 14; Samuel G. Hanson, Anil K Kashyap, and Jeremy C. Stein, "A Macro-prudential Approach to Financial Regulation," *Journal of Economic Perspectives* 25, no. 1 (2011): 3–28.

446. Ben Bernanke, "Reducing Systemic Risk" (speech, Federal Reserve Bank of Kansas City's Annual Economic Symposium, Jackson Hole, WY, August 22, 2008). Lehman Brothers filed for bankruptcy less than one month later, on September 15, 2008.

447. House Committee on Banking, Finance and Urban Affairs, "Inquiry into Continental Illinois Corp. and Continental Illinois National Bank," Hearings before the House Subcommittee on Financial Institutions Supervision, Regulation and Insurance, 98th Cong., 2nd sess., September 18, 1984, p. 214 (emphasis added).

448. House Committee on Banking, Finance and Urban Affairs, "Inquiry into Continental Illinois Corp.," p. 216 (emphasis added).

449. Conover's testimony also contradicts the notion that federal regulators were hamstrung because they were unable to obtain the proper information from each other. Conover testified: "I would say, first of all, that we have the tools to get the information that we need. Do we need any new enforcement powers or tools of that nature? I honestly don't think so . . . but we have cease-and-desist powers, civil money penalty powers, authority to remove officers." House Committee on Banking, Finance and Urban Affairs, "Inquiry into Continental Illinois Corp.," p. 338.

450. John P. LaWare, member, Board of Governors of the Federal Reserve System, Testimony before the Subcommittee on Economic Stabilization of the House Committee on Banking, Finance, and Urban Affairs, 102nd Cong., 1st sess., May 9, 1991, p. 12.

451. LaWare, Testimony, p. 14.

452. Federal Reserve Board of Governors, "Uniform Financial Institutions Rating System," news release, December 24, 1996. The FDIC formally adopted the new system in 1997. Federal Deposit Insurance Corporation, "Uniform Financial Institutions Rating System," Notice of Adoption of Policy Statement, 62 Fed. Reg. 752 (Jan. 6, 1997).

453. The proposal is a joint rule issued by all three federal banking regulators. The notice of the proposal states, "Historical experience has demonstrated the

impact *individual banking organizations* can have on the stability of the U.S. banking system, in particular banking organizations that would have been subject to the proposal" (emphasis added). Office of the Comptroller of the Currency, Department of the Treasury, Board of Governors of the Federal Reserve System, and Federal Deposit Insurance Corporation, "Regulatory Capital Rule: Large Banking Organizations and Banking Organizations with Significant Trading Activity," Notice of Proposed Rulemaking, 88 Fed. Reg. 64030 (Sept. 18, 2023).

454. See 12 US Code § 3907. Ultimately, the federal agencies jointly decided to use the Basel requirements as their guidelines for what constitutes adequate capital.

455. House Committee on Banking, Finance and Urban Affairs, "Inquiry into Continental Illinois Corp.," p. 219.

456. Paul H. Kupiec, "Basel III: Some Costs Will Outweigh the Benefits," American Enterprise Institute *Financial Services Outlook*, November 2013.

457. For more on the risk-bucket approach, see Howard D. Crosse, *Management Policies for Commercial Banks* (Englewood Cliffs, NJ: Prentice-Hall, 1962), pp. 169–72.

458. See Jeffrey Friedman and Wladimir Kraus, *Engineering the Financial Crisis: Systemic Risk and the Failure of Regulation* (Philadelphia: University of Pennsylvania Press, 2011), p. 69.

459. Michel and Ligon, "Basel III Standards Do Not Reduce Too-Big-to-Fail Problem."

CHAPTER 7

460. Joe Weisenthal, "The 4 Things That Worry Jamie Dimon . . .," *Business Insider*, February 4, 2013. Dimon was far from alone. Before the law was enacted, the CEO of investment banking giant Goldman Sachs, Lloyd Blankfein, welcomed more regulation, saying, "The biggest beneficiary of reform is Wall Street itself." Vicki Needham, "Blankfein Supports Financial Reform Bill," *The Hill*, April 27, 2010. Blankfein also said, "We will be among the biggest beneficiaries of reform." Tim Carney, "Goldman CEO: 'We Will Be among the Biggest Beneficiaries of Financial Reform,'" *Washington Examiner*, May 4, 2010.

461. Robert Kaiser, "'Act of Congress': How Barney Frank Foiled the Banking Lobby to Form a New Financial Watchdog," *Washington Post*, May 5, 2013. Section 331 of Dodd-Frank changed the FDIC's assessment base for deposit insurance fees paid by banks. Rather than pay fees based on total deposits, banks now had to pay on the basis of their average consolidated total assets minus their average tangible equity (effectively total liabilities). The change requires banks that pose higher risks to the economy (larger banks) to pay higher rates.

Raj Gnanarajah, "FDIC's Deposit Insurance Assessments and Reserve Ratio," Congressional Research Service, August 24, 2018.

462. Peter Schroeder, "Cuts to SEC Would Imperil the Market, Says Finance Sector," *The Hill*, February 9, 2011.

463. Schroeder, "Cuts to SEC Would Imperil the Market."

464. Charles W. Calomiris and Stephen H. Haber, *Fragile by Design: The Political Origins of Banking Crises and Scarce Credit* (Princeton, NJ; Princeton University Press, 2014), p. 13.

465. Federal backing for losses, whether during so-called emergencies or even in normal times, is a topic largely beyond the scope of this book. Nonetheless, federal backing in financial markets must be pared back along with the core regulatory changes discussed in this chapter. For more, see Norbert Michel, "Title XI Does Not End Federal Reserve Bailouts," in *The Case against Dodd-Frank: How the "Consumer Protection" Law Endangers Americans* (Washington: Heritage Foundation, 2016), pp. 169–79; George Selgin, "Reforming Last Resort Lending," in *Prosperity Unleashed: Smarter Financial Regulation*, ed. Norbert Michel (Washington: Heritage Foundation, 2017), pp. 201–12; and Diane Katz, "The Massive Federal Credit Racket," in *Prosperity Unleashed, pp. 179–200.*

466. For example, in the University of Washington's Milliman Lecture, Nobel Laureate Robert Lucas told his audience, "A fractional reserve banking system will always be fragile, a house of cards." George Selgin, "Fatalistically Flawed: A Review Essay on *Fragile by Design*, by Charles W. Calomiris and Stephen H. Haber," *International Finance 18*, no. 1 (2015): 109–28. Many scholars argue that both banking and financial intermediation are inherently unstable. Chicago School economists Henry Simons and Lloyd Mints are just two examples. George Selgin, "Are Banking Crises Free-Market Phenomena?," *Critical Review* 8, no. 4 (1994): 591. Also see Tony Saunders, Marcia M. Cornett, and Otgo Erhemjamts, *Financial Markets and Institutions*, 8th ed. (New York: McGraw Hill, 2022), p. 17.

467. For a more general discussion of these theories, see Calomiris and Haber, *Fragile by Design, pp. 480–84.*

468. Although it is like a basic spillover argument, others argue that regulation is necessary to protect the *payments system.* That is, it is needed to protect people's ability to use their accounts to conduct transactions. John P. LaWare, member, Board of Governors of the Federal Reserve System, Testimony before the Subcommittee on Economic Stabilization of the House Committee on Banking, Finance, and Urban Affairs, 102nd Cong., 1st sess., May 9, 1991.

469. Morgan Ricks and Lev Menand, "Scrap the Bank Deposit Insurance Limit," *Washington Post*, March 15, 2023. In his book, Ricks equates all money market instruments to "cash equivalents," thus arguing that this entire financial segment should be regulated as banks, and explicitly backed by the government,

because it is engaged in money creation. Ricks, *The Money Problem: Rethinking Financial Regulation* (Chicago: University of Chicago Press, 2016).

470. Omarova withdrew from the nomination process amid controversy over her interventionist views on the financial industry, which some critics likened to communist economic policies. Pete Schroeder and Andrea Shalal, "Omarova Withdraws Nomination to Lead U.S. Office of the Comptroller of the Currency," Reuters, December 7, 2021.

471. Saule Omarova, "The People's Ledger: How to Democratize Money and Finance the Economy," *Vanderbilt Law Review* 74, no. 5 (2021): 1232. Saule Omarova, "Banks Can't Be Trusted: A 'Golden Share' Might Help," *New York Times*, March 23, 2023.

472. Omarova, "The People's Ledger," p. 1299. Similarly, Ricks, Menand, and another scholar believe that giving Americans accounts at the Federal Reserve would offer an "astonishing range" of benefits, including "greater financial and macroeconomic stability." Morgan Ricks, John Crawford, and Lev Menand, "Fed-Accounts: Digital Dollars," *George Washington Law Review* 951 (2021): 125.

473. Norbert Michel, "Gruenberg Speech Exposes Flaws in Financial Stability Mandate," *Forbes*, October 4, 2023; Norbert Michel, "McKernan Underscores Problems with FDIC's Systemic Risk Exception," *Forbes*, May 16, 2023.

474. George Kaufman, "Bank Contagion: A Review of the Theory and Evidence," *Journal of Financial Services Research* 8, no. 2 (1994): 143.

475. The first two reasons are examples of what economists refer to as a "moral hazard," a type of situation where people take higher than normally expected risk because they believe they will not suffer the consequences associated with possible losses from taking the higher risk. The third reason is an example of what economists refer to as a "Hayekian knowledge problem," named after Nobel Prize–winning economist F. A. Hayek. Hayek, "The Use of Knowledge in Society," *American Economic Review* 35, no. 4 (1945): 519–30.

476. Hyman Minsky, for example, theorized that private markets are inherently unstable and prone to "wide and spreading bankruptcies," and require a "big government and alert lender of last resort" to stave off such problems. Hyman Minsky, "The Financial-Instability Hypothesis: Capitalist Processes and the Behavior of the Economy," *Hyman P. Minsky Archive* 282 (1982), p. 13.

477. It is true that federal backing helped quell a panic during the Great Depression, and that there have been fewer bank runs after the FDIC was created. But even ignoring the federal policies that caused such turmoil in the US banking sector before the Depression (and beyond), it does not automatically follow that the federal government should insure bank deposits. Indeed, it is very easy to argue that the creation of the FDIC has prevented better private solutions for insuring deposits from arising. George Selgin, "The New Deal and Recovery, Part 27: Deposit Insurance," *Alt-M*,

March 28, 2023; Thomas L. Hogan and Kristine Johnson, "Alternatives to the Federal Deposit Insurance Corporation," *Independent Review* 20, no. 3 (2016): 433–54; Mark Carlson and Kris James Mitchener, "Branch Banking as a Device for Discipline: Competition and Bank Survivorship during the Great Depression," *Journal of Political Economy* 117, no. 2 (2009): 165–210; Norbert Michel and David Burton, "Financial Institutions: Necessary for Prosperity," Heritage Foundation Backgrounder no. 3108, April 14, 2016, pp. 12–13.

478. The approach has spread to the payments sector and beyond. For instance, a recent US Treasury report calls for the federal government to "establish a federal framework for payments regulation to protect users and the financial system, while supporting responsible innovations in payments." US Department of the Treasury, *The Future of Money and Payments* (Washington: US Department of the Treasury, 2022), p. 2. Similarly, a recent Federal Reserve policy statement says, "The Board's objectives are to foster the safety and efficiency of payment, clearing, settlement, and recording systems (collectively known as financial market infrastructures [FMIs]), and to promote financial stability more broadly." Federal Reserve Board of Governors, "Federal Reserve Policy on Payment System Risk," July 21, 2023.

479. Graham Steele, "Confronting the 'Climate Lehman Moment': The Case for Macroprudential Climate Regulation," *Cornell Journal of Law and Public Policy* 30, no. 1 (2020): 155.

480. Steele, "Confronting the 'Climate Lehman Moment,'" p. 156. The approach regulators use to implement many of the Dodd-Frank Act's new responsibilities is often referred to as "macroprudential" regulation.

481. Steele, "Confronting the 'Climate Lehman Moment,'" p. 142.

482. Steele, "Confronting the 'Climate Lehman Moment,'" pp. 148, 150–51 (emphasis added).

483. For more on regulatory discretion, see Norbert Michel, David Burton, and Nicolas Loris, "Using Financial Regulation to Fight Climate Change: A Losing Battle," Heritage Foundation Backgrounder no. 3634, June 24, 2021.

484. Kelsey Bolar, "Unsealed Choke Point Documents Show Obama Was Far from Scandal-Free," *Daily Signal*, October 16, 2018. Also see Federal Deposit Insurance Corporation, Office of the Inspector General, "The FDIC's Role in Operation Choke Point and Supervisory Approach to Institutions That Conducted Business with Merchants Associated with High-Risk Activities," OIG Report no. AUD-15-008, September 2015, p. 12.

485. Douglas Landy and Glen R. Cuccinello, "A New "Operation Choke Point"? The Quickly Changing Rules on Crypto Activities for Member Banks," White & Case LLP, February 14, 2023; David Z. Morris, "The Reality behind the Crypto Banking Crackdown: 'Operation Choke Point 2.0' Is Here," *Consensus Magazine*, March 22, 2023.

486. These principles were previously used in Michel, *The Case against Dodd-Frank* and *Prosperity Unleashed*. For a brief list of regulatory reforms, see Nicholas Anthony et al., *Sound Financial Policy: Principled Recommendations for the 118th Congress*, ed. Norbert Michel and Ann Rulon (Washington: Cato Institute, 2022).

487. Emily Ekins, "Cato Institute 2022 Financial Regulation National Survey," August 2022. A previous version of this survey reports similar results. Emily Ekins, "Wall Street vs. the Regulators: Public Attitudes on Banks, Financial Regulation, Consumer Finance, and the Federal Reserve," Cato Institute, September 19, 2017.

Index

Information in figures is indicated by *f*; n designates a numbered note.

entry restrictions, with banks, 82
Equal Credit Opportunity Act of 1974
    (ECOA), 90–91*f*
equity markets. *See* securities markets
examination, with banks, 82, 84–85
exchange-traded funds (ETFs), 55–56,
    163n186, 164n195
external finance, 15

Fair Credit Reporting Act of 1970
    (FCRA), 90–91*f*
Fannie Mae, 5, 52, 131, 181n376
FDIC. *See* Federal Deposit Insurance
    Corporation (FDIC)
FDICIA. *See* Federal Deposit
    Insurance Corporation
    Improvement Act of 1991
    (FDICIA)
Federal Deposit Insurance Act of
    1950, 83–84
Federal Deposit Insurance
    Corporation (FDIC), 26, 81, 83,
    86–89, 96, 124, 134, 172n290,
    175n323, 187n452, 188n461,
    190n477
Federal Deposit Insurance
    Corporation Improvement Act
    of 1991 (FDICIA), 89
Federal Financial Institutions
    Examination Council (FFIEC),
    173n292
Federal Home Loan Bank Board, 89
Federal Home Loan Banks, 24, 122,
    175n326
Federal Reserve
    real bills doctrine and, 167n257
    in regulation, 85, 88, 103, 122
    repurchase agreements and, 50–51
Federal Reserve Act of 1913, 24
Federal Savings and Loan Insurance
    Corporation (FSLIC), 89, 124

FFIEC. *See* Federal Financial
    Institutions Examination
    Council (FFIEC)
Financial Crimes Enforcement
    Network, 97
financial crisis of 2008. *See* Great
    Recession
financial firms
    bank holding companies and, 83
    banks vs., 38
    Dodd-Frank and, 87
    Federal Deposit Insurance
        Corporation Improvement Act
        and, 117
    functions of, 34–38
    in segments, 38–40
Financial Industry Regulatory
    Authority (FINRA), 45, 97, 99,
    178n348
financial institutions, types of,
    40–46
Financial Institutions Reform,
    Recovery, and Enforcement
    Act of 1989 (FIRREA), 89,
    175n326
Financial Institutions Supervisory Act
    of 1966, 88
financial instruments, 46–62
financialization, 168n263
financial markets
    economic growth and, 8, 14–17
    government as dominating, 5
    historical overview of, 7–29
    as inseparable from American
        prosperity, 77–79
    love-hate relationship with,
        17–27
    overview of modern, 31–62
    popular myths about, 27–29
    primary, 38–40, 44
    secondary, 33–34, 38–40, 44
    as vital, 34–38

About the Authors

Norbert J. Michel is vice president and director of the Cato Institute's Center for Monetary and Financial Alternatives, where he specializes in issues pertaining to financial markets and monetary policy. Michel is the author of *Why Shadow Banking Didn't Cause the Financial Crisis: And Why Regulating Contagion Won't Help.*

Jennifer J. Schulp is the director of financial regulation studies at the Cato Institute's Center for Monetary and Financial Alternatives, where she focuses on the regulation of securities and capital markets. She has testified before Congress multiple times, including before the US Senate Committee on Banking, Housing, and Urban Affairs and the US House Committee on Financial Services.

About the Cato Institute

Founded in 1977, the Cato Institute is a public policy research foundation dedicated to broadening the parameters of policy debate to allow consideration of more options that are consistent with the principles of limited government, individual liberty, and peace. The Institute is named for *Cato's Letters*, libertarian pamphlets that were widely read in the American colonies in the early 18th century and played a major role in laying the philosophical foundation for the American Revolution.

The Cato Institute undertakes an extensive publications program on the complete spectrum of policy issues. Books, monographs, and shorter studies are commissioned to examine the federal budget, Social Security, regulation, military spending, international trade, and myriad other issues. Major policy conferences are held throughout the year.

The Cato Institute's Center for Monetary and Financial Alternatives was founded in 2014 to assess the shortcomings of existing monetary and financial regulatory arrangements, and to discover and promote more stable and efficient alternatives.

In order to maintain its independence, the Cato Institute accepts no government funding. Contributions are received from foundations, corporations, and individuals, and other revenue is generated from the sale of publications. The Institute is a nonprofit, tax-exempt, educational foundation under Section 501(c)3 of the Internal Revenue Code.

CATO INSTITUTE
1000 Massachusetts Ave. NW
Washington, DC 20001
www.cato.org